50

68

76

99

editor's letter

I'm always amazed at how this magazine business works. Just when I think we can't possibly top our last efforts, here comes another cookbook with brand new recipes, gorgeous photos, and dishes that actually taste *better* than they look. And that's exactly what you'll find in this *Splendid Soups* publication.

Granted, soup is a fairly friendly topic to explore. I mean, who doesn't like it? Its simplicity in preparation *and* presentation is part of its broad appeal. Plus, soup knows no season—it's great year-round (even in the summer!). But maybe its best quality is that it works for one person as easily as it does for ten. Not many dishes out there can make that claim.

So what's in store for you here? A lot. From classic *old-fashioned chicken noodle*, to more complex-tasting *chicken and crab callaloo*, to the unique *cheeseburger*, these soups are flavor-packed and fun to make. And we take them a step further: Each splendid soup includes an appropriate side or "extra," transforming what's normally just a "course" in a meal to the main attraction—without any guesswork. For example, *beer cheese soup* is paired with bratwurst and pumpernickel skewers, and the *easy, cheesy broccoli soup* comes with apple-walnut salad. How cool is that?

I could go on and on about how great the recipes are, but you'll find out soon enough. Most were created with three things in mind: your schedule, your health, and easy-to-get ingredients. There are a few indulgent recipes, but in general, cream is added sparingly, pureeing is used to thicken, and fats are minimal.

Enjoy *Splendid Soups*. You'll find the recipes as unique as they are delicious.

John Meyer

FLAVOR ENHANCED BROTH

Yes, homemade broth is best, but enhanced store-bought broth is good too. A little time and a few ingredients are all you need.

chicken broth

There's the old school of thought that says nothing compares to homemade broth. Perhaps, but what's wrong with taking a box or can of good broth and making it just a little bit better?

This process isn't hard at all. The cool part is that the vegetables don't even need peeling or stemming...just wash them well and chop coarsely.

Now, here are a few things you need to keep in mind when enhancing chicken broth. First, only simmer it for about an hour. Also, make sure it's a *simmer*, not a boil—cooking it too long or hard will turn the broth cloudy. And finally, when the broth is done simmering, strain it gently (no pressing). This, too, will cloud the stock.

Enhanced Chicken Broth

Makes about 7 cups; Total time: 1½ hours

SIMMER:

8	cups purchased chicken broth
2	lb. chicken wings, rinsed
2	cups leeks, chopped, rinsed
1	cup celery, chopped
1	cup carrot, chopped
½	cup fresh parsley (including stems)
6–8	whole black peppercorns

Simmer all ingredients in a large pot over medium heat for 1 hour, skimming off any impurities from the top (avoid boiling the stock—impurities will turn it cloudy); strain.

beef broth

For the most part, canned beef broth tastes beefy, but that's about all. To enhance it, simply add a few ingredients to fortify it and bring out other flavors.

Now, the key to good home-made beef stock is browning the bones and vegetables. Since this is just "enhanced," no bones are used, but the vegetables are browned to develop deeper flavor. To do this, saute them in oil to start caramelization, then coat with tomato paste and roast in the oven. This two-step process intensifies the tomato flavor, deepens the broth's color, and removes the raw taste from the paste. Finally, add the packaged stock and simmer in the oven.

Enhanced Beef Broth

Makes about 7 cups; Total time: 2½ hours

SAUTE IN 2 T. OLIVE OIL:

2	cups onion, chopped
1	cup celery, chopped
1	cup carrot, chopped
1	cup mushrooms, chopped
4	garlic cloves, smashed

STIR IN AND ROAST:

2	T. tomato paste

ADD:

8	cups purchased beef broth
1	T. Worcestershire sauce
8–10	whole black peppercorns
1	bay leaf

Preheat oven to 350°.

Saute vegetables and garlic in oil in a large ovenproof pot over medium-high heat. Cook until vegetables begin to brown, about 15 minutes, stirring occasionally.

Stir in tomato paste to coat the vegetables. Transfer to the oven and roast for 1 hour.

Add broth and remaining ingredients. Cover, return pot to the oven, and roast 1 hour. Remove from the oven, let cool, then strain.

broth review

There's no need to feel guilty about using purchased chicken broth, especially if you make an educated choice. Here are our picks.

Let's face it—not all of us have the time (or energy!) to make homemade stock for soup. Cooking shortcuts are always welcome, though, and using boxed or canned broth does trim time in the kitchen.

However, the choices are vast, so we tested our way through several brands to narrow the playing field a bit. Each one you see here works fine for any of the soups in this book. But every brand also has its idiosyncrasies that may affect the choice you make. For instance, one requirement for me is low sodium—salt can be added to the soup as desired. I also steer clear of those with MSG, and prefer the flavor of broth from a box ("aseptic" packaging) over a can. But, again, let your own preferences be your guide.

FOND DE POULET
This highly reduced "perfect chicken stock" is intensely flavored with no salty aftertaste, chemicals, preservatives, MSG, or sugar. One drawback is that it's only available via mail order.

CAMPBELL'S
This canned broth's excellent chicken flavor surprised me. One minus—it has added MSG and a slightly tinny taste. It's condensed, so you need to add water.

MANISCHEWITZ
This is the only broth I found that is certified kosher. Because it's condensed, you'll need to adjust with water and taste for strength.

KITCHEN BASICS
This broth has a dark, rich color and roasted vegetable flavor without MSG, fat, or gluten. It also has less sodium than most brands tested. Its only problem is the color—some soups made with it were oddly "beefy" looking.

SWANSON

We use Swanson's "Natural Goodness" line in the test kitchen a lot, and it's hard to beat for overall flavor, color, and versatility. The organic broth is good, but cloudy, and the 99% fat free canned broth was lacking a bit of body.

COLLEGE INN

College Inn broth has pretty good flavor, but its regular broth is fairly high in sodium (the "light" version is within reasonable range). It's not always easy to find, however.

IMAGINE ORGANIC

The Imagine brand of broths are all certified organic. The *free range* variety (good chicken flavor) works better for soups than the *cooking stock* (heavy onion taste).

PACIFIC ORGANIC

If you want great chicken flavor in a *very* low sodium (70mg/cup) broth, Pacific is a good choice. It can be hard to find, but natural food stores are most likely to carry it.

BUTTERBALL

The name Butterball is synonymous with turkeys, so it's no surprise to see their name on chicken broth too. The flavor of this broth was fine, but it's got added MSG.

summer garden
VEGETABLE

Coercing your family (or yourself!) to eat more vegetables just got easier. With this soup and fluffy herb dumplings, you won't have to twist arms too hard.

We all could probably stand to eat more vegetables, and this produce-packed soup makes the task so much easier! One unusual twist to this recipe is the herb dumplings. They give the perfect amount of substance to the vegetable-laden broth. The dumplings are cooked separately, not in the soup, to ensure that they don't overcook or turn the soup broth cloudy. Poach them in chicken or vegetable broth or water.

The vegetables go into the soup in different stages to accommodate their varying cooking times. Follow the procedure carefully so you don't have mushy cauliflower swimming with crunchy green beans.

Summer Garden Vegetable Soup

Makes 13 cups

Saute onion, carrot, and celery (called mirepoix) in oil to begin developing the flavor base.

Add potatoes, cauliflower, and zucchini to the broth. They take a little while to cook.

The tomatoes, corn, beans, and okra go in at the end—they don't need as much cooking time.

Total time: 45 minutes

SAUTE IN 2 T. OLIVE OIL:
1   cup onion, diced
1/2   cup carrot, diced
1/2   cup celery, diced

DEGLAZE WITH; STIR IN:
1/2   cup dry white wine
6   cups chicken or vegetable broth
2   cups small red potatoes, quartered
2   cups cauliflower florets
1   cup zucchini, diced
1   bay leaf

ADD:
3   cups tomatoes, diced
2   cups fresh or frozen corn kernels
1   cup fresh green beans, trimmed
1   cup fresh or frozen okra, sliced
    Salt and pepper to taste

Saute onion, carrot, and celery in oil in a large pot over medium heat. Cook for 5 minutes, or until vegetables begin to soften.

Deglaze with wine; simmer until nearly evaporated. Stir in broth, potatoes, cauliflower, zucchini, and bay leaf. Bring to a boil, reduce heat, and simmer 10 minutes.

Add tomatoes, corn, beans, okra, salt, and pepper. Return to a boil and cook 5 more minutes.

Per cup: 109 calories; 29% calories from fat; 4g total fat; 15g carb.; 90mg sodium; 3g fiber; 4g protein

Adding **ON**

Herb Dumplings

Makes 20–25 dumplings
Total time: 30 minutes

WHISK TOGETHER AND STIR IN; MELT:
1 1/2   cups all-purpose flour
3   T. Parmesan, grated
2 1/2   t. baking powder
1   t. sugar
1   t. kosher salt
1/2   t. ground black pepper
1/4   cup chopped fresh chives
1/4   cup chopped fresh parsley
2/3   cup whole milk
3   T. unsalted butter

HEAT; COOK DUMPLINGS IN:
    Simmering water, chicken broth, or vegetable broth

Whisk flour, Parmesan, baking powder, sugar, salt, and pepper together in a bowl; stir in the herbs. Melt butter in the milk in a saucepan over medium heat, then blend into dry ingredients; stir just until moistened. Shape dough into balls the size of ping pong balls.

Heat enough water or broth in a saute pan to come 1" up the side. Add dumplings, cover, and gently simmer 10 minutes, or until a toothpick inserted in the center comes out clean.

Per 2 dumplings: 101 calories; 36% calories from fat; 4g total fat; 13g carb.; 282mg sodium; 1g fiber; 3g protein

Soup**TIP**

Light, fluffy dumplings are one of life's great comfort foods. The dumplings for this recipe are easy to make and take very little time. Just be sure not to overmix, keep the liquid at a simmer during cooking, and don't crowd the pan—the dumplings need room to expand.

black bean soup

Rich, thick, and full of flavor, black bean soup is a "full-body" classic. Serve it with fresh pico de gallo and spicy pork kebabs for an over-the-top meal.

The beauty of this black bean soup is that it turns out great, even with canned beans. The secret is in what I like to call "layers of flavor." Take a look at the recipe—see how something flavorful is added in nearly every step? From the bay leaves to coriander to the sofrito [soh-FREE-toh], a sauteed mixture of onion, herbs, and spices, this soup is piled high with great tasting stuff.

If you want even more flavor (and aren't opposed to a little meat in the dish), saute 2–3 strips of diced bacon, remove it, then cook the sofrito in the drippings. Add the bacon bits to the soup at the end.

Black Bean Soup

Makes 8 cups

Remove half the bean mixture and puree what remains in the pot. Be sure to remove the bay leaf first.

Add garlic to the onion mixture (the "sofrito"), stirring frequently to prevent the garlic from burning.

Add vinegar to the sofrito—it will brighten the flavor of the mixture rather than make it sour.

Total time: about 1 hour

SIMMER:

4   cans black beans, rinsed, drained (15 oz. each)
6   cups chicken broth
1   bay leaf

PUREE:

     Half the beans and broth

SAUTE IN 2 T. OLIVE OIL:

1   cup white onion, diced
2   T. garlic, minced
1   T. paprika
1½   t. ground cumin
1½   t. dried oregano
1   t. ground coriander
½   t. cayenne
     Pinch each of sugar and salt

DEGLAZE WITH; ADD:

1   T. red wine vinegar
1   can diced tomatoes in juice (15 oz.)

SERVE WITH:

     Pico de Gallo, *Page 95*

Simmer beans and broth in a large pot over medium heat for 20–30 minutes. Remove bay leaf and half of the bean-broth mixture.

Puree the remaining bean mixture in the pot with a hand-held stick blender or in a food processor until smooth. Return reserved beans to the pot; keep warm over low heat.

Saute onion, garlic, and seasonings in oil in a nonstick skillet until soft, about 5 minutes.

Deglaze pan with vinegar, then add tomatoes and their juice. Simmer to reduce slightly, then mash tomatoes lightly. Add to soup and cook another 5 minutes.

Serve with pico de gallo.

Per cup: 261 calories; 22% calories from fat; 7g total fat; 35g carb.; 882mg sodium; 12g fiber; 15g protein

SoupTIP

Canned beans make this soup very easy to pull together, but cooking dried beans gives you more control over the salt content. Simply simmer 1 lb. of black beans in water or broth until tender, about 1 hour.

Adding ON

Spiced Pork Kebabs

Makes 8 kebabs; Total time: 30 minutes

COMBINE:

1   t. brown sugar
1   t. chili powder
1   t. kosher salt
½   t. ground black pepper
¼   t. cayenne

THREAD; GRILL

1   lb. pork tenderloin, trimmed and cut into 1½–2" pieces
½   lb. kielbasa, cut diagonally into 1"-thick slices

Preheat a grill or a grill pan on the stove to medium-high.

Combine sugar and spices in a small bowl.

Thread 2 chunks of pork and 1 piece of kielbasa on each of 8 skewers. Sprinkle with the spices and grill until pork is cooked through, 6–8 minutes per side.

Per kebab: 177 calories; 60% calories from fat; 12g total fat; 2g carb.; 530mg sodium; 0g fiber; 15g protein

butternut
squash SOUP

Think the only way to prepare squash is to bake it with butter and brown sugar?

Not so. Simmered in broth and pureed smooth, squash makes a dynamite soup.

It's hard to believe that rock-hard butternut squash could turn into something so smooth and creamy once it's cooked. But it's just the ticket for a rich pureed soup.

Amazingly enough, the squash can be pureed after just about 20 minutes of simmering. To be sure it's tender, taste-test three or four cubes. There must not be any crunchiness, or it won't puree properly.

I have to admit, one of my favorite things about this soup is its garnish of Romesco Sauce, *Page 96*. This Spanish condiment of roasted red peppers and almonds is the perfect contrast to the smooth soup.

Butternut Squash Soup

Makes 8 cups

Add the sage to the onions—if fresh isn't available, use 1 teaspoon dried sage (not ground) instead.

Pour the brandy into the onion mixture and simmer briefly to allow the onions to absorb its flavor.

Stir in the squash, then the broth and wine. Simmer until squash is tender enough to pierce with a fork.

Total time: about 1 hour

SAUTE IN 2 T. EACH OLIVE OIL AND UNSALTED BUTTER:

1	cup onion, diced
1	T. garlic, minced
2	t. minced fresh sage
1	t. sugar
1/2	t. red pepper flakes
1/8	t. ground cinnamon

STIR IN; ADD:

1/4	cup brandy
8	cups butternut squash, peeled, seeded, cut into 1" chunks
4	cups chicken broth
1	cup dry white wine

FINISH WITH:

1/4	cup heavy cream
	Salt and pepper to taste

TOAST; SPRINKLE WITH AND BROIL:

8	baguette slices, toasted
1	cup Gruyere cheese, shredded Romesco Sauce, *Page 96*

Saute onion, garlic, sage, sugar, pepper flakes, and cinnamon in oil and butter in a large pot over medium heat. Cook until onion is soft, about 10 minutes.

Stir brandy into the onion mixture and cook for 1 minute; add the squash, broth, and wine. Bring to a boil, reduce heat, partially cover, and simmer until squash is tender, about 20 minutes. Working in batches, puree soup in a blender. Return soup to the pot.

Finish soup with cream, salt, and pepper. Preheat broiler to High.

Toast baguette slices on a baking sheet under the broiler; sprinkle with cheese, then broil again to melt cheese, 1–2 minutes. Top each serving of soup with a baguette and drizzle with Romesco Sauce.

Per cup: 360 calories; 55% calories from fat; 22g total fat; 20g carb.; 362mg sodium; 1g fiber; 10g protein

Adding **ON**

Sausage-Apple Empanadas

Makes 8 empanadas; Total time: 40 minutes

SAUTE AND ADD; DEGLAZE WITH:

1/4	lb. bulk Italian sausage
1/3	cup Braeburn apple, diced
2	T. pecans, chopped
1	T. dry sherry
	Salt and pepper to taste

BEAT; ROLL OUT AND FILL:

1	egg
1	T. water
1	sheet puff pastry, thawed

SPRINKLE WITH:

	Grated Parmesan and paprika

Preheat oven to 400°; line a baking sheet with parchment paper.

Saute sausage in a skillet over medium-high heat until brown, 3–4 minutes. Add the apple and pecans, then deglaze with sherry, cooking until nearly evaporated, about 2 minutes. Season the mixture; chill while preparing the dough.

Beat the egg and water together for the egg wash; set aside. Roll the pastry sheet out on a floured work surface to a 13" square. With a pizza wheel, cut the pastry into 8 triangles as if cutting a pizza.

Fill each triangle with a heaping tablespoon of chilled sausage mixture. Brush edges with egg wash, fold in half to enclose filling, and crimp edges closed with a fork. Place empanadas on the prepared baking sheet; brush with egg wash. **Sprinkle with** cheese and paprika, and bake until golden, about 15 minutes.

Per empanada: 87 calories; 57% calories from fat; 6g total fat; 4g carb.; 169mg sodium; 1g fiber; 5g protein

Soup**TIP**

To prepare the squash, first very carefully halve it lengthwise with a long-bladed knife. Scoop out the seeds and stringy parts attached to the flesh, then cut each half in half again. Remove skin with a vegetable peeler and slice squash into cubes. (See Page 19 for pureeing tips.)

greek lentil SOUP

Leave any preconceived "health food" notions you may have about lentils at the kitchen door. This soup is as flavorful as it is nutritious.

Does lentils' healthy image leave a bad taste in your mouth? Then try this soup. After a spoonful, you may change your tune—being virtuous has never tasted so good!

There are lots of lentil varieties out there, *see right*, but for this, try finding quick-cooking red lentils. Soaking them in hot water beforehand speeds the cooking process even more. If you can't find them, the everyday olive green-colored lentils work fine, but need to simmer longer to soften fully. To test for doneness, don't eat just one lentil, eat several. Depending on their age, cooking times may vary.

Greek Lentil Soup

Makes 7 cups

Soak lentils in boiling water for 20 minutes. This will keep them from getting too mushy during cooking.

Add the tomatoes and bring to a boil—you may use fresh or canned tomatoes for this soup.

Stir in drained lentils, return soup to a simmer, and cook just until lentils are soft. Add spinach.

Total time: 50 minutes

SOAK IN 8 CUPS BOILING WATER:
1½   cups dried red lentils

SAUTE IN 3 T. OLIVE OIL:
2   cups onion, diced
1   T. garlic, minced
1   T. minced fresh oregano
1   bay leaf

DEGLAZE WITH; ADD:
¼   cup lemon juice
6   cups vegetable broth
2   cups tomatoes, seeded, diced

STIR IN:
        Soaked red lentils
4   cups fresh spinach, chopped
        Salt and pepper to taste

Soak lentils in the water in a large bowl. Cover and let stand 20 minutes, then drain and set aside.

Saute onion and garlic in oil in a large pot over medium-high heat until soft, 4–5 minutes. Add oregano and bay leaf; cook 1 minute.

Deglaze with lemon juice and reduce until nearly evaporated. Add broth and tomatoes, bring to a boil, reduce heat to low, and simmer 10 minutes. Remove bay leaf.

Stir in lentils and simmer until lentils are soft but not mushy, about 10 minutes. Add spinach and cook 1 minute to wilt; season with salt and pepper.

Per cup: 259 calories; 26% calories from fat; 7g total fat; 38g carb.; 963mg sodium; 10g fiber; 15g protein

Adding **ON**

Pita Triangles
with feta yogurt dip

Makes 24 chips, about ⅓ cup sauce
Total time: 25 minutes

FOR THE DIP—
COMBINE:
½   cup plain yogurt
½   cup feta cheese, crumbled
2   T. fresh lemon juice
2   T. olive oil
        Salt and pepper to taste

FOR THE TRIANGLES—
HALVE CROSSWISE:
2   pocket-style pitas

WHISK TOGETHER; BRUSH PITA WITH:
½   cup olive oil
1   t. ground turmeric
1   t. ground cumin
1   t. ground cardamom
½   t. dried oregano leaves
¼   t. cayenne
¼   t. kosher salt

Preheat oven to 375°.

Combine yogurt, feta, lemon juice, oil, salt, and pepper for the dip. Chill until ready to serve.

Halve each pita crosswise (through the "pocket") to make 4 rounds.

Whisk oil and spices together and brush on cut sides of pita halves. Cut each circle into 6 wedges, arrange on a baking sheet, and bake 7–9 minutes, or until crisp. Watch carefully—chips tend to brown at different rates.

Per 4 chips with 1½ T. sauce: 311 calories; 77% calories from fat; 27g total fat; 13g carb.; 331mg sodium; 1g fiber; 4g protein

SoupTIP

The most common lentil on grocery store shelves is the split pea-size, olive-colored lentil. French green lentils are smaller, rounder and streaked with black. Red lentils are even tinier and cook quickly (use them for this). Find them in natural food, gourmet, or ethnic food stores.

tuscan minestrone

Minestrone means "big soup" in Italian, and this one is enormous in two ways—body and flavor. It's so chunky, you'll be tempted to dive in with a fork.

Forget any notion of the watery, insipid minestrones you may have encountered in the past. This recipe puts them to shame, all due to a couple of simple steps.

First, the vegetables are treated a little differently here than in other soups. The "sturdy" ones, like onions and carrots, are sweated as you might expect. But the zucchini and spinach get sauteed separately to help retain color and texture. It may seem fussy, but it's a step worth doing.

Second, olive oil plays a key role in the soup's flavor so use one of good quality—extra-virgin is great, but virgin works too.

Tuscan Minestrone

Makes 8½ cups

Sweat onions, fennel, celery, carrots, and garlic until soft. The vegetables should not turn brown.

While soup simmers, saute zucchini. This way, the color won't fade as it would if simmered in the broth.

Ladle soup over some of the sauteed spinach, then finish with olive oil, Parmesan, and pepper.

Total time: about 1 hour

SWEAT IN 3 T. OLIVE OIL; STIR IN:

2	cups onion, sliced
2	cups fennel bulb, sliced
1	cup celery, sliced
1	cup carrot, sliced
4	garlic cloves, smashed
4	cups chicken broth
1	can diced tomatoes in juice (14½ oz.)

SAUTE IN 1 T. OLIVE OIL;
ADD TO SOUP:

1	cup zucchini, sliced
1	can cannellini beans, drained and rinsed (15 oz.)
2	T. Basil Parsley Pesto, *Page 97*
	Salt and red pepper flakes to taste

SAUTE IN BATCHES IN 1 T. OLIVE OIL:

4	cups fresh spinach

GARNISH WITH:

Extra-virgin olive oil
Parmesan cheese curls
Freshly ground black pepper

Sweat onion, fennel, celery, carrot, and garlic in 3 T. oil in a large pot over medium-high heat; cook until soft, about 10 minutes. Stir in broth and tomatoes, and bring to a boil. Reduce heat and simmer, partially covered, for 20 minutes.

Saute zucchini in 1 T. oil in a nonstick skillet over medium-high heat. Add zucchini to the soup along with the beans, pesto, salt, and red pepper flakes; simmer 5 minutes.

Saute the spinach in two batches in 1 T. oil in the same skillet used for the zucchini; add more oil as needed. Divide spinach between serving bowls, then ladle soup on top.

Garnish by drizzling soup with olive oil, then top with curls of Parmesan and black pepper.

Per cup: 222 calories; 50% calories from fat; 12g total fat; 22g carb.; 455mg sodium; 7g fiber; 8g protein

Adding **ON**

Open-face Grinders

Makes 4 grinders; Total time: 15 minutes

HALVE LENGTHWISE; DRIZZLE WITH:

2	ciabatta sandwich rolls
	Purchased Italian dressing or olive oil and red wine vinegar

DIVIDE AMONG ROLLS; BROIL:

6	oz. thinly sliced assorted cured meats, such as salami, ham, and mortadella
2	slices provolone cheese

Preheat broiler to High.
Halve the rolls, then drizzle the cut sides with dressing.
Divide meats and cheese among each roll half, then arrange on a baking sheet. Broil until cheese melts and is golden brown, about 3 minutes. Slice in half diagonally and serve.

Per grinder: 328 calories; 58% calories from fat; 21g total fat; 18g carb.; 412mg sodium; 1g fiber; 17g protein

roasted tomato SOUP

Life is full of choices. You can either eat a $30.00 steak or a $3.00 soup

and sandwich—not a tough decision if it's tomato soup and grilled cheese.

There's something special about tomato soup, especially if it's homemade *and* ultra easy to make! This soup's great flavor comes from oven-roasting the tomatoes, which enhances their sweetness and adds a flavor dimension that stewing does not. No need to use broth for depth—just add water!

Pureeing the soup not only smooths out the texture, it also smooths out its flavor. But be cautious, *see Tip box, right.* Pureeing hot soup can be dangerous. Don't fill the carafe too full and be sure to cover the lid with a towel. Steam can build up inside, so start at low speed and work your way up.

Roasted Tomato Soup

Makes 10 cups

Use your hands to toss the tomatoes, garlic, and oil. This way you can feel them to coat evenly.

Include all the juice from the roasted tomatoes when adding to the onions—it provides a ton of flavor.

Puree the soup in batches in a blender (see Tip below). A handheld stick blender works too.

Total time: about 1 hour

Toss Together; Roast:
- 5 lb. tomatoes, stemmed and quartered
- 6 garlic cloves, smashed
- 1/4 cup olive oil
  Salt and black pepper

Saute in 2 T. Olive Oil; Stir in:
- 1 cup onion, chopped
- 2 cups water
- 2 t. sugar
- 1/2 t. kosher salt
- 1/4 t. red pepper flakes
  Roasted tomato mixture

Finish with; Garnish with:
- 1/2 cup heavy cream
  Sprigs of fresh basil

Preheat oven to 450°.

Toss tomatoes, garlic, 1/4 cup oil, salt, and pepper in a bowl. Transfer to a casserole dish and roast about 40 minutes, or until very soft.

Saute onion in 2 T. oil in a large pot over medium heat 5–7 minutes. Stir in water, sugar, salt, pepper flakes, and roasted tomato mixture. Bring to a boil, reduce heat, and simmer, 10 minutes. Puree the soup in a blender until smooth.

Finish soup with cream and garnish each serving with a basil sprig.

Per 1 1/4 cups: 286 calories; 76% calories from fat; 24g total fat; 17g carb.; 153mg sodium; 3g fiber; 3g protein

Adding **ON**

Pesto-Mozzarella Dippers

Makes 4 sandwiches
Total time: 20 minutes

Spread and Layer:
- 8 slices crusty Italian bread, 1/2" thick
- 4 T. unsalted butter, softened, divided
- 8 t. Basil Parsley Pesto, *Page 97*, divided
- 6 oz. fresh mozzarella, sliced, divided

Spread butter on one side of each slice of bread; spread 1 teaspoon pesto on the other side. On 4 of the bread slices, arrange the cheese on the pesto in a single layer. Cover the cheese with the remaining bread slices, buttered side up.

Heat a nonstick griddle or skillet over medium for 2 minutes. Grill the sandwiches 2–3 minutes, or until golden underneath. Turn the sandwiches, press firmly with a spatula, and cook 2–3 minutes more, or until bread is toasted and cheese is melted. Turn once more, press, and cook 30 seconds. Remove from heat and let stand 3 minutes so cutting is easier.

Per sandwich: 308 calories; 69% calories from fat; 24g total fat; 11g carb.; 308mg sodium; 1g fiber; 10g protein

Soup**TIP**

Many soups in this book are pureed, making them smooth, rich, and creamy. A blender does the job well, but don't fill it more than halfway and wrap a dish towel around the lid to prevent splattering. Start on low speed, then gradually increase speed one increment at a time.

classic
FRENCH ONION soup

There is a reason that French Onion is one of the most well-known soups in the world—it simply tastes amazing. Period.

Even if you're not an onion fan, good onion soup can transcend almost any aversion to them. While most of the ingredients just go together naturally, the key to a good onion soup is caramelizing the onions. This means cooking them slowly until the natural sugars turn a deep, rich brown.

Sweet varieties, like Vidalia, Walla Walla, or Maui, make a milder soup. But I prefer a bolder flavor, so I use a mixture of yellow and red onions, which are available year-round. And while true onion soup is made with veal stock, I've found that a chicken-beef broth blend works just fine.

Classic French Onion Soup

Makes 9½ cups

Stir the onions and garlic together, then cover and sweat for 10 minutes. Cook until caramelized.

Adding flour adds body and thickens the broth. Coat the onions well, stirring often to prevent scorching.

Finish the soup with a toasted crouton and a generous sprinkling of both cheeses, then broil.

Total time: about 1½ hours

SWEAT IN ¼ CUP OLIVE OIL, THEN CARAMELIZE:
2   *each* yellow, white, and red onions, sliced (12 cups)
¼   cup garlic, minced

ADD AND REDUCE:
1   cup dry white wine
⅓   cup dry sherry

STIR IN; ADD AND SIMMER:
3   T. all-purpose flour
3   cups chicken broth
3   cups beef broth
    Bundle of fresh thyme
    Salt and pepper to taste

TOAST; TOP SOUP WITH AND BROIL:
8   slices baguette, toasted (½" thick)
1   cup Gruyere cheese, shredded
½   cup Parmesan, shredded

Sweat onion and garlic in oil, covered, over medium heat in a large pot for 10 minutes. Uncover and cook 40 minutes, or until onions are caramelized, stirring occasionally.

Add wine and sherry, then increase heat to high. Cook until wine evaporates, stirring often.

Stir in flour and cook 1 minute. Add both broths, thyme, salt, and pepper; bring to a simmer and cook 10 minutes more. Meanwhile, preheat broiler to High.

Toast baguette slices on a baking sheet under the broiler. Ladle soup into ovenproof bowls, arrange on the baking sheet, then top with a toasted baguette. Sprinkle with some of the cheeses, then broil 1–2 minutes, or until cheese melts.

Per cup: 293 calories; 46% calories from fat; 15g total fat; 21g carb.; 302mg sodium; 2g fiber; 12g protein

Soup**TIP**

When I say "crouton" here, I'm not talking about a cube of stale bread, but rather a slice of toasted French bread. Croutons are critical to good onion soup. Yes, they taste wonderful in it, but their real purpose is to keep the cheese afloat for easy browning (called gratinée).

Adding **ON**

Classic Vinaigrette Salad

Makes 8 cups salad, ⅔ cup vinaigrette
Total time: 15 minutes

WHISK TOGETHER:
¼   cup red wine vinegar
3   T. olive oil
1   T. shallot, minced
1   T. Dijon mustard
1   t. sugar
    Salt and pepper to taste

TOSS VINAIGRETTE WITH:
4   cups soft lettuces, such as Boston or Bibb
4   cups mesclun salad mix
4   radishes, sliced
2   T. chopped fresh basil

Whisk first seven ingredients together in a bowl.

Toss lettuces, radishes, and basil with enough dressing to coat. (Leftover dressing may be chilled for up to 1 week.)

Per cup: 35 calories; 71% calories from fat; 3g total fat; 2g carb.; 21mg sodium; 1g fiber; 1g protein

red bean & chard SOUP

What do you get when you pack a lot of good-for-you vegetables into one pot?

A knock-out soup that'll have you eating seconds—and maybe even thirds!

I don't think any more color could go into a soup than what you see here. With beans, greens, pasta, and vegetables, it's a full meal deal—even without meat!

Swiss chard is an underutilized winter green that adds incredible color, texture, and flavor to this soup. I cook the stems and leaves separately; since the stems are slightly fibrous, they need a bit more cooking time in the soup than the leaves do.

Ditalini [dih-tah-LEE-nee] is a small pasta about the size of corn kernels. If you can't get your hands on ditalini, orzo or pennette make fine substitutes.

Red Bean and Chard Soup

Makes 9 cups

Total time: 45 minutes

Saute the diced chard stems with the onion and carrot. They add celery-like texture, flavor, and color.

Cook the pasta separately, then add it to the soup. This way, it won't absorb too much of the broth.

Saute the chard leaves before adding them to the soup—it will help retain their brilliant green color.

SAUTE IN 3 T. OLIVE OIL:

2	cups onion, diced
1	cup Swiss chard stems, diced
1/2	cup carrot, diced
1	t. garlic, minced
1	t. chopped fresh rosemary
1/4	t. red pepper flakes

DEGLAZE WITH; STIR IN:

1/2	cup dry white wine
6	cups chicken broth
2	cups tomatoes, chopped
3	cups cooked ditalini or other small pasta (1½ cups dry)
1	cup canned red kidney beans, drained and rinsed
	Salt and pepper to taste

SAUTE IN 1 T. OLIVE OIL:

8	cups Swiss chard leaves, chopped, rinsed, and dried (1 bunch)

GARNISH WITH:

Grated Parmesan

Saute onion, chard stems, carrot, garlic, and seasonings in 3 T. oil in a large pot over medium-high heat; cook for 5 minutes.

Deglaze with wine and reduce until nearly evaporated. Stir in broth and tomatoes, and bring to a boil. Reduce heat and simmer 5–7 minutes, then add the cooked pasta, beans, salt, and pepper.

Saute chard leaves in 1 T. oil in a large saute pan over medium-high heat. Cook until wilted, season with salt, then add to the soup.

Garnish servings of soup with grated Parmesan.

Per cup: 285 calories; 29% calories from fat; 9g total fat; 36g carb.; 380mg sodium; 5g fiber; 13g protein

Adding **ON**

Caprese Salad

Makes 3 cups; Total time: 10 minutes

TOSS TOGETHER:

3	cups ripe tomatoes (such as Campari or Romanita), halved or quartered (about 12 tomatoes)
1	cup fresh mozzarella, cubed
3	T. extra-virgin olive oil
2	T. fresh lemon juice
1	T. thinly sliced fresh basil
	Salt and pepper to taste

Toss all ingredients together and serve immediately.

Per 1/2 cup: 133 calories; 76% calories from fat; 11g total fat; 4g carb.; 62mg sodium; 1g fiber; 4g protein

wild mushroom soup

Classic flavors dominate this recipe—woodsy mushrooms, rich cream, smoky sherry, and dill make this vegetable soup flavorful enough to satisfy any appetite.

There are certain things that can make or break mushroom soup. Here are a couple of elements to think about so yours turns out mouth-wateringly delicious.

First, using a combination of mushrooms will provide a good variety of flavors and textures. Grocery stores carry more kinds of cultivated "wild" mushrooms than ever before, so here's your shot at trying some new ingredients. Second, while I consider dill to be a fairly strong, sometimes overpowering herb, use it here. Its flavor is quite refreshing and offsets some of that earthy taste that mushrooms harbor.

Wild Mushroom Soup

Makes 7 cups   Total time: about 1 hour

Mushrooms give off a lot of moisture as they cook. Be sure to saute until all the liquid is evaporated.

Stir in the sherry to deglaze the pan, stirring up the brown particles on the bottom—they're full of flavor.

After simmering, stir in the cornstarch mixture. The soy sauce enhances the mushrooms' flavor.

PREPARE:

2	lb. assorted mushrooms (button, crimini, and shiitake), sliced

SAUTE IN 2 T. EACH UNSALTED BUTTER AND OLIVE OIL:

1	cup onion, minced
2	garlic cloves
	Prepared mushrooms

STIR IN; ADD:

1/4	cup dry sherry
1	T. fresh lemon juice
1	T. paprika
1/2	t. ground black pepper
4	cups chicken broth

WHISK TOGETHER; STIR IN:

2	T. cornstarch
2	T. soy sauce

FINISH WITH:

1/2	cup heavy cream
1	T. chopped fresh dill
	Salt to taste

GARNISH WITH:

Sour cream
Lemon slices
Additional chopped fresh dill

Prepare button and crimini mushrooms, slicing in a food processor using the thick slicing disk. For the shiitakes, trim off stems and discard, then thickly slice the caps, *see below*.

Saute onion and garlic in oil and butter in a large pot over medium-high heat. Cook 5 minutes, or until soft, stirring often. Add mushrooms, increase heat to high, and saute until moisture evaporates. Reduce heat to medium.

Stir in sherry, lemon juice, paprika, and pepper. Simmer until sherry has nearly evaporated, then add broth. Increase heat to high, bring to a boil, reduce heat to medium-low, and simmer gently for 20 minutes.

Whisk cornstarch and soy sauce together to dissolve, then stir into simmering soup to thicken.

Finish with cream, dill, and salt.

Garnish with sour cream, lemon slices, and fresh dill.

Per cup: 201 calories; 66% calories from fat; 15g total fat; 12g carb.; 188mg sodium; 2g fiber; 6g protein

SoupTIP

Shiitake mushrooms have tough stems which should be removed and discarded before using. For the best texture in the soup, slice the caps into thick pieces.

Adding ON

Risotto Alfredo

Makes about 3 cups
Total time: 35 minutes

HEAT:

4	cups chicken broth

SAUTE IN 2 T. UNSALTED BUTTER:

1	cup onion, diced

STIR IN; ADD:

1	cup medium grain rice
1/4	cup dry white wine
	Warm broth

OFF HEAT, FINISH WITH:

1/4	cup Parmesan, grated
1/4	cup heavy cream
	Salt and pepper to taste
	Chopped fresh chives

Heat broth in a saucepan over medium just until hot. Reduce heat to low and keep warm.

Saute onion in butter in a large saute pan over medium heat. Cook 3 minutes, or until slightly soft.

Stir in rice and cook 2 minutes, stirring constantly. Add wine, stirring until absorbed, then add the warm broth, stirring occasionally until liquid is absorbed and rice is tender, about 20 minutes.

Off heat, finish with Parmesan, cream, seasonings, and chives.

Per 1/2 cup: 210 calories; 27% calories from fat; 6g total fat; 30g carb.; 161mg sodium; 1g fiber; 7g protein

Spanish GAZPACHO

Gazpacho was made for the dog days of summer. They've come and gone now, but make this recipe next year!

I'll admit, cold soups have never been my thing. But this gazpacho [gahz-PAH-choh] has won me over. Its cooling impact is most evident in the summer, when it's hot out and vegetables are super-fresh (and coming out your ears!). Plus, how can you not like a soup that doesn't require using the stove?

The base here is actually V-8 juice. Easy! And the vegetables can be prepared in the food processor (but you can certainly do them by hand). Smoked paprika, *see Tip, right*, is really something in this, but if you can't find it, regular paprika is fine—be sure it's a fairly new jar for maximum flavor.

Gazpacho

Makes 11 cups

Add the smoked paprika to the tomato juice base, and whisk it together well to combine.

Pulse the vegetables coarsely, but finely mince the onion, parsley, and garlic before adding to the soup.

Grate the carrots, add them to the soup, and refrigerate for an hour to allow flavors to blend and mellow.

Total time: 20 minutes + chilling

COMBINE AND CHILL:

1	bottle V-8 juice (46 oz.)
1/2	cup red wine vinegar
2	T. fresh lemon juice
2	T. olive oil
1	T. Worcestershire sauce
1	t. smoked paprika
1	t. Tabasco
	Salt and pepper to taste

PULSE SEPARATELY; ADD:

3	cups tomatoes, seeded, chopped
2	cups cucumber, chopped
2	cups celery, chopped
2	cups yellow bell pepper, chopped
1/2	red onion, chopped
1/2	cup chopped fresh parsley
1	garlic clove
1/2	cup carrot, grated

SERVE SOUP WITH:

Benedictine Sandwiches, *right*
Herb Grilled Shrimp Kebabs, *Page 93*

Combine V-8, vinegar, lemon juice, oil, Worcestershire, paprika, Tabasco, salt, and pepper in a large bowl.
Pulse the tomatoes in a food processor until fairly fine but still a bit chunky; add to the V-8 base. Then individually pulse the cucumber, celery, and bell pepper; add each to the base. Pulse the onion, parsley, and garlic together and stir into the soup along the carrots. Chill gazpacho until cold, at least 1 hour (soup keeps 2–3 days refrigerated).
Serve bowls of chilled gazpacho with sandwiches and shrimp skewers, if desired.

Per cup: 73 calories; 34% calories from fat; 3g total fat; 10g carb.; 349mg sodium; 2g fiber; 2g protein

Adding **ON**

Benedictine Sandwiches

Makes 8 sandwiches; Total time: 20 minutes

PULSE; DRAIN:

1/2	cup cucumber, seeded, chopped
2	T. onion, chopped
2	t. chopped fresh mint

ADD:

4	oz. cream cheese, softened
	Salt to taste

SPREAD MIXTURE ON; GARNISH WITH:

8	baguette slices, toasted
	Parsley leaves

Pulse cucumber, onion, and mint in a food processor until minced. Press in a fine-mesh strainer to remove excess water; return pulp to the processor bowl.
Add cream cheese and puree until smooth; season with salt.
Spread mixture on toasted baguette; garnish with parsley.

Per sandwich: 79 calories; 61% calories from fat; 5g total fat; 9g carb.; 100mg sodium; 0g fiber; 2g protein

Soup**TIP**

Smoked paprika adds a delightfully smoky flavor to food. That smokiness comes from chile peppers that have been dried over burning oak. If possible, buy it from a reputable spice retailer—they tend to carry the most flavorful varieties, plus they rotate their stock regularly.

OLD-FASHIONED
chicken noodle

Of **course** your grandma's chicken noodle soup is the best, but after you try this

soul-comforting version, you may never go back. Your secret is safe with us.

This chicken noodle soup is as simple as it gets, but a little extra TLC has gone into it, which really pays off in terms of flavor.

First of all, roasting the chicken rather than boiling it adds a lot of dimension to the broth, as does the sweet, subtle onion essence of the leeks. Second, try to get your hands on kluski noodles, *see Page 29*. Why? Well, they're a bit thicker than ordinary egg noodles and give the soup a more old-fashioned quality. Finally, don't omit the garnish of fresh herbs and lemon wedges—they add just the right amount of liveliness to the finished soup.

Old-Fashioned Chicken Noodle Soup

Makes 13 cups

While the roasted chicken cools slightly, prepare the vegetables and get them simmering in the broth.

Remove chicken from the bones and add to soup along with any pan juices from roasting.

Add kluski noodles off heat. Cover and let stand until tender to prevent the noodles from overcooking.

Total time: 2¼ hours

ROAST:

1 whole chicken, seasoned with salt and pepper (3–4 lb.)

BRING TO A BOIL; STIR IN; SIMMER:

8 cups chicken broth
2½ cups celery, sliced
1½ cups carrot, sliced
1½ cups leeks, sliced into half-moons, rinsed thoroughly
   Shredded chicken pieces and juices from the pan

ADD:

8 oz. kluski noodles

STIR IN; SERVE SOUP WITH:

¼ cup chopped fresh parsley
   Lemon wedges

Preheat oven to 450°.
Roast chicken on a rack in a roasting pan for 1 hour, or to an internal temperature of 165° in the thigh. Remove from the oven and let rest 15–20 minutes. When cool enough to handle, remove meat from the bones in large pieces.
Bring the broth, celery, carrot, and leeks to a boil in a large pot over high heat. Reduce heat to medium and simmer gently for 5 minutes. Stir in chicken pieces and any juices from the roasting pan; simmer 5 more minutes.
Add noodles, cover pot, and remove from heat. Let stand for 15 minutes, then eat a noodle to test for doneness. If they're still slightly undercooked, replace lid, and let stand an additional 3–5 minutes, or until fully tender.
Stir in parsley and serve soup with lemon wedges.

Per 1½ cups: 324 calories; 30% calories from fat; 11g total fat; 29g carb.; 281mg sodium; 2g fiber; 28g protein

Adding **ON**

Avocado-Tomato Melts

Makes 8 halves; Total time: 10 minutes

TOAST; TOP AND SEASON WITH:

4 English muffins, split
1 ripe avocado, pitted, peeled, and sliced
2 Roma tomatoes, thinly sliced
   Salt and pepper

SPRINKLE WITH:

1 cup farmer cheese, shredded
¼ cup Parmesan, shredded

Preheat broiler to High.
Toast muffin halves on a baking sheet under the broiler until golden. Top with avocado and tomato, then season with salt and pepper.
Sprinkle each muffin with both cheeses and broil 2–3 minutes, or until melted.

Per ½ English muffin: 229 calories; 31% calories from fat; 8g total fat; 17g carb.; 230mg sodium; 3g fiber; 8g protein

Soup**TIP**

"Kluski" is a generic Polish term for all types of dumplings, but sometimes also refers to any variety of noodles. For this, I used a dry kluski noodle found in the grocery store aisle with the dried pastas. But if you can't find them, any dry or frozen egg noodle will work.

chicken mulligatawny

This soup has it all—a little sweetness, a touch of spiciness, and tons of texture from chicken and fruit salsa. Here's a dish that's as much fun to eat as it is to say!

In southern India, mulligatawny means "pepper water," but don't let that keep you away from this soup. You'd be missing out on one of the best! Yes, it's spicy, but it's very controllable—if you prefer to tame things down, just scale back the "volatile" elements, like the curry powder, jalapeño, and red pepper flakes. Plus, the coconut milk and side dishes of lightly sweetened rice and fruit salsa help buffer the heat.

Not sure when you purchased your jar of curry powder? You may want to invest in a new one. Old curry has no punch and will do nothing to enhance the soup's flavor.

Chicken Mulligatawny Soup

Makes about 9 cups

Total time: 1¼ hours

Brown the chicken (it's not necessary to cook it through), then remove it from the pot.

Saute onion, curry powder, and seasonings briefly to help cook out the "raw" flavor in the spices.

Make a roux [ROO] with butter and flour, whisk in strained soup, then add it back to the soup to thicken.

BROWN IN 3 T. VEGETABLE OIL:

2   lb. boneless, skinless chicken thighs, cut into 2" pieces, seasoned with salt and pepper

ADD AND SAUTE:

1   cup onion, diced
3   T. curry powder
3   T. fresh ginger, minced
2   T. garlic, minced
2   jalapeños, seeded, minced
½   t. red pepper flakes

STIR IN; SIMMER:

4   cups chicken broth
1   cup tomatoes, seeded, diced
¼   cup chopped fresh cilantro
     Reserved chicken

MELT; WHISK IN:

2   T. unsalted butter
2   T. all-purpose flour
2   cups strained soup broth

FINISH SOUP WITH; GARNISH WITH:

2   cups fresh spinach, chopped
1   can coconut milk (14 oz.)
     Toasted coconut

Brown chicken in oil on all sides in a large pot over medium-high heat; transfer to a plate.

Add onion, curry powder, ginger, garlic, jalapeño, and red pepper flakes to the pot; saute 3 minutes.

Stir in broth, tomatoes, cilantro, and reserved chicken. Bring to a boil, reduce heat to medium, and simmer 10 minutes. Remove and strain enough of the soup broth out to measure 2 cups (return any strained out solids to the pot). Set the strained liquids aside.

Melt the butter in a saucepan over medium heat, then whisk in the flour to make a roux. Gradually add the strained soup, simmer for 1 minute, then whisk the mixture into the pot of soup. Simmer 2–3 minutes to thicken and cook out the floury taste.

Finish with spinach and coconut milk, and garnish with coconut.

Per cup: 363 calories; 60% calories from fat; 24g total fat; 11g carb.; 201mg sodium; 3g fiber; 27g protein

SoupTIP

Stir the spinach leaves into the simmering soup, then turn off the heat. Spinach wilts in less than a minute, giving you time to dish up the rice and salsa.

Adding ON

Coconut Rice & Salsa

Makes about 3 cups rice, 3 cups salsa
Total time: 20 minutes

FOR THE RICE—
BRING TO A BOIL; STIR IN:

1½   cups water
1   cup canned coconut milk
2   t. sugar
1   t. kosher salt
1   cup basmati or jasmine rice

FINISH WITH:

2   T. fresh lime juice
1   T. unsalted butter

FOR THE SALSA—
TOSS TOGETHER:

1   mango, peeled, pitted, diced
1   Granny Smith apple, diced
     Juice of 1 lime

Bring water, coconut milk, sugar, and salt for the rice to a boil in a saucepan over medium-high heat. Stir in rice, cover, reduce heat to low, and cook 15 minutes. Remove from heat; let stand for 5 minutes.

Finish rice with lime juice and butter. Fluff with a fork and keep warm.

Toss all ingredients for the salsa together in a bowl; serve on top of the soup with rice on the side.

Per ½ cup rice and ½ cup salsa: 186 calories; 48% calories from fat; 10g total fat; 25g carb.; 326mg sodium; 2g fiber; 2g protein

Italian Wedding
SOUP

Classic Italian flavors unite in this satisfying, yet surprisingly light-tasting soup. White wine, rich broth, creamy beans, and hearty meatballs—the combination is a match made in heaven!

There are plenty of flavors you'll recognize in this great Italian soup—garlic, white wine, oregano, and red pepper, to name a few. But this bowl of flavor doesn't really step up to the plate until the meatballs gently simmer in the broth. Without a doubt, this adds a totally different, but delightful, dimension.

Besides the meatballs, there are two other ingredients that really make this soup pop. Fresh spinach is stirred in and briefly cooked. In my book, any time you add spinach to a dish, it's a winner. Then, right at the end, whisk in beaten eggs—it's a great trick for enhancing the soup's richness, color, and body.

Italian Wedding Soup

Makes about 10 cups

Deglaze sweated vegetables and ham with wine, then simmer until nearly evaporated.

Drop meatballs into the simmering soup and cook just until they float to the top.

Stir the egg-broth mixture into the soup off heat. The residual heat is enough to cook the eggs.

Total time: 1 hour

ASSEMBLE:
1 recipe Italian Mini Meatballs, *right*

SWEAT IN 2 T. OLIVE OIL:
1 cup onion, diced
1 cup celery, diced
1 cup carrot, diced
1 cup ham, diced
1 T. garlic, minced

DEGLAZE WITH; STIR IN AND SIMMER:
1/2 cup dry white wine
6 cups chicken broth
2 t. dried oregano
2 t. red pepper flakes
1 bay leaf

DROP IN; ADD:
   Prepared meatballs
1 can cannellini beans, drained and rinsed (15 oz.)
2 cups fresh spinach
1/2 cup chopped fresh flat-leaf parsley

WHISK TOGETHER; ADD:
2 eggs
   Hot soup broth

GARNISH WITH:
   Shredded Parmesan

Assemble meatballs and set aside.
Sweat vegetables, ham, and garlic in oil in a large pot, covered, over medium heat until soft, 10 minutes.
Deglaze with wine; reduce until nearly evaporated. Stir in broth and seasonings, bring to a boil, reduce heat, and simmer 15–20 minutes.
Drop meatballs into simmering soup and cook gently until they float, 3–4 minutes. Add beans, spinach, and parsley, and cook just until the spinach wilts, about 2 minutes.
Whisk eggs with some of the hot broth, then remove the soup from the heat; stir in the egg mixture.
Garnish soup with Parmesan.

Per 1¼ cups: 277 calories; 42% calories from fat; 13g total fat; 19g carb.; 839mg sodium; 5g fiber; 20g protein

Adding **ON**

Italian Mini Meatballs

Makes 30 walnut-size meatballs
Total time: 15 minutes

STIR TOGETHER:
1/4 cup unseasoned fresh bread crumbs
1/4 cup Parmesan, grated
2 T. whole milk
2 T. chicken broth
2 T. chopped fresh flat-leaf parsley
1 egg, beaten
2 t. dried Italian seasoning
1 t. garlic, minced
1 t. kosher salt
1/2 t. ground black pepper
1/4 t. red pepper flakes
   Pinch nutmeg

ADD:
1/2 lb. ground chuck

Stir all ingredients together (except the ground chuck) in a large mixing bowl.
Add the chuck and mix thoroughly. Form meatballs using a small scoop or melon baller and place on a parchment-lined baking sheet; chill until ready to use.

Per meatball: 20 calories; 40% calories from fat; 1g total fat; 1g carb.; 95mg sodium; 0g fiber; 2g protein

SoupTIP

The eggs add richness and a creamy texture to the soup. Be sure to whisk them together well with a little bit of the hot broth. This is called "tempering," and will help prevent the eggs from curdling when added to the hot soup.

split pea with ham

Split pea soup is wonderful; however, looks aren't its strong suit. This one changes all that—great taste and good looks. You can't go wrong.

The key to great split pea soup starts with the right ratio of liquid to peas. If too much liquid is added, the soup will be watery, and if too little is used, the soup ends up thick and gloppy. In this recipe, the right amount of sherry, broth, and water, plus a little blending, make for perfect texture.

But flavor isn't sacrificed for texture— aromatic vegetables sauteed in butter provide a great-tasting base, which is built up with plenty of dried and fresh herbs. Whole strips of bacon (they're removed later) add subtle smokiness, and chunks of ham give the soup plenty of meaty texture.

Split Pea and Ham Soup

Makes 7½ cups

Add sherry to the vegetables and reduce. Allowing it to evaporate helps concentrate its sweet flavor.

Rinse the split peas to remove any dirt and sand, then add them to the simmering broth mixture.

Add the frozen peas and ham to the soup. Simmer until peas are cooked but still green, about 5 minutes.

Total time: 1½ hours

FOR THE SOUP—

SWEAT IN 1 T. UNSALTED BUTTER:

1	cup onion, diced
1	cup celery, diced
1	cup carrot, sliced

DEGLAZE WITH; ADD:

¼	cup dry sherry
4	cups chicken broth
2	cups water
1	cup green split peas, rinsed
2	strips thick-sliced bacon
2	t. fresh thyme leaves
1	bay leaf

STIR IN:

2	cups frozen green peas
2	cups ham, diced
½	cup minced fresh parsley
2	T. unsalted butter, *optional*
	Salt and pepper to taste

FOR THE CREMA—

COMBINE:

½	cup sour cream
1	T. lemon zest, minced
1	T. minced fresh mint

Sweat onion, celery, and carrot in butter for the soup in a large pot, covered, over medium-high heat. Cook 3–4 minutes, or until vegetables are soft.

Deglaze with sherry; reduce until nearly evaporated. Add broth, water, split peas, bacon, and seasonings. Bring to a boil, reduce heat to medium-low, and simmer, partially covered, 50–60 minutes, or until peas are tender. Remove bacon and bay leaf, then puree 2 cups of soup in a blender; return the pureed mixture to the pot.

Stir in frozen peas, ham, parsley, butter (if using), salt, and pepper.

Combine sour cream, zest, and mint for the crema in a bowl. Garnish soup with a dollop of crema and sprig of mint if desired.

Per 1¼ cups: 415 calories; 39% calories from fat; 18g total fat; 37g carb.; 709mg sodium; 4g fiber; 25g protein

SoupTIP

For a treat, use fresh shell peas from the farmers market in place of the frozen peas; one pound yields about 1 cup shelled peas. If making the wraps, right, buy pasteurized crabmeat. It's expensive but has better flavor and texture than the canned crab found in the tuna aisle.

Adding **ON**

Crab Salad Wraps

Makes 4 wraps; Total time: 15 minutes

TOSS TOGETHER:

1	can pasteurized crabmeat, (6½ oz.)
1	avocado, pitted, peeled, diced
¼	cup "Special Sauce" Dressing, *Page 69*
	Salt and pepper to taste

DIVIDE CRAB SALAD BETWEEN:

4	soft lettuce leaves, such as Boston or Bibb

GARNISH WITH:

½	cup tomatoes, diced

Toss crab, avocado, and "Special Sauce" Dressing together in a bowl; season with salt and pepper.

Divide salad among lettuce leaves, filling as you would a taco.

Garnish with tomatoes.

Per wrap: 188 calories; 70% calories from fat; 15g total fat; 7g carb.; 245mg sodium; 4g fiber; 10g protein

chicken PHO GA

Have it your way—the phrase pertains not only to fast food burgers but to this soup too! With pho, it's never been easier to "do your own thing."

This soup is different every time I make it—and I use the same recipe! But Vietnamese pho [FUH] isn't so much about how it's cooked but about how it's "embellished." Many of the ingredients (herbs, noodles, vegetables) are on the side for people to add to their bowls as they please. So depending on what goes in, it's different every time.

For this, it's critical to make your own broth; purchased stuff *won't* do. But it's a simple job. Just be sure to skim the broth as it simmers to achieve crystalline clarity.

Chicken Pho Ga

Makes 8 cups

Start by making a flavorful broth with chicken wings, onions, celery, ginger, and garlic; simmer 3 hours.

To keep the broth clear, skim off fat and foam from the surface. And don't boil—it clouds the broth.

Strain the broth, then add the chicken, onion, carrot, and scallions, and simmer briefly.

Total time: about 4 hours

SIMMER AND SKIM; STRAIN AND SEASON WITH:

10	cups water
4	lb. chicken wings
2	onions, quartered
2	cups celery, leaves and ribs, chopped
1	piece of fresh ginger, chopped (8")
6	garlic cloves, smashed
	Salt to taste

ADD:

12	oz. boneless skinless chicken breast, thinly sliced
1	cup red onion, thinly sliced
1	cup carrot, shredded
1/2	cup scallions, green part only, thinly sliced

SERVE WITH:

7	oz. rice vermicelli, softened
1/2	cup fresh basil leaves
1/2	cup fresh cilantro leaves
1/2	cup fresh mint leaves
2	cups bean sprouts, rinsed
1/2	cup jalapeño or serrano chile, sliced
1	lime, cut into wedges

Simmer water, chicken wings, onion, celery, ginger, and garlic in a large pot for 3 hours. As the broth simmers, skim off any foam that rises to the top. Strain the broth through a fine-mesh sieve; discard the solids. Return the broth to the pot, season with salt, and bring back to a simmer.

Add the chicken, onion, carrot, and scallions. Simmer soup about 10 more minutes, or until chicken is cooked through.

Serve bowls of broth, chicken, and vegetables with noodles, herbs, sprouts, chiles, and lime wedges on the side for adding as desired.

Per cup: 221 calories; 26% calories from fat; 6g total fat; 27g carb.; 100mg sodium; 2g fiber; 13g protein

SoupTIP

Rice vermicelli (banh pho) is slightly transparent, very brittle, and must be soaked in boiling water for 10 minutes before using. During soaking, it turns milky white and becomes soft and slippery. Find it in the Asian section of grocery stores or at Asian markets.

Adding ON

Mini Spring Rolls

Makes 8 spring rolls, 1/2 cup sauce
Total time: 30 minutes

FOR THE PEANUT SAUCE—
PUREE:

1/4	cup fresh lime juice
1/4	cup creamy peanut butter
1/4	cup sugar
1	T. chili garlic sauce
2	t. soy sauce

FOR THE SPRING ROLLS—
PREPARE:

3/4	cup cooked cellophane noodles
1/3	cup napa cabbage, shredded
1/4	cup carrot, sliced into strips
1/4	cup shiitake mushrooms caps, thinly sliced
1	T. torn fresh mint leaves

SOFTEN IN HOT WATER; FILL:

8	spring roll wrappers (6")

Puree all ingredients for the sauce in a blender until smooth; set aside.

Prepare noodles, vegetables, and mint for the spring rolls; set aside.

Soften wrappers one at a time (so they don't stick together) in hot water until pliable, about 30 seconds. Lay the softened wrapper on a cutting board or damp towel and arrange some noodles, cabbage, carrot, mushrooms, and mint in the center; roll as a burrito. Assemble remaining rolls and serve with sauce for dipping.

Per spring roll with 1 T. sauce: 165 calories; 23% calories from fat; 4g total fat; 30g carb.; 105mg sodium; 1g fiber; 4g protein

tomato & turkey
TORTELLINI

After a day or two, turkey leftovers tend to lose their luster. But this tomatoey, pasta-packed soup shines them up beautifully.

Turkey soup recipes are a dime a dozen. But look closely before breezing by this one—it's got features worth checking out.

First, the base is made from roasted tomatoes. Grocery stores carry many sweet varieties (Campari, Romanita), which are great, but grape or cherry are fine too.

Second, fresh cheese tortellini is a delicious addition. Precook the pasta before adding it to the soup. This way, it won't overcook and get too soft.

Finally, if making the cheese crisps, *right*, use inexpensive grated Parmesan. And a nonstick pan is an absolute must.

Tomato Tortellini with Roast Turkey Soup

Makes 8 cups

Stir the seasoned tomatoes, onions, and garlic with enough olive oil to coat before roasting.

Additional broth will give the thick roasted tomato sauce a thinner, more soup-like consistency.

Cook the tortellini separately, then add it to the soup just to heat through to keep it "al dente."

Total time: 1 hour

COMBINE, TOSS WITH, AND ROAST:

8	cups Campari or Romanita tomatoes, quartered
1	cup onion, coarsely chopped
4	garlic cloves
2	t. kosher salt
1	t. sugar
1	t. red pepper flakes
1/2	cup olive oil

COOK:

1	pkg. fresh cheese tortellini (9 oz.)

BRING TO A BOIL; STIR IN:

	Roasted tomato mixture
2	cups chicken broth
2	cups cooked turkey or chicken, chopped
	Prepared tortellini

SERVE WITH:

Parmesan Crisps, *below*
Fresh basil

Preheat oven to 450°.

Combine tomatoes, onion, garlic, salt, sugar, and pepper flakes in a shallow roasting pan or large casserole dish. Toss with oil and roast 35–40 minutes, or until tomatoes are soft. Remove tomatoes from the oven and mash with a potato masher, keeping them a bit chunky, then transfer to a large pot.

Cook tortellini according to package directions; drain and set aside.

Bring tomato mixture to a boil with the broth. Stir in the turkey and tortellini; simmer just until heated through.

Serve with Parmesan Crisps and fresh basil.

Per cup: 341 calories; 49% calories from fat; 19g total fat; 27g carb.; 656mg sodium; 3g fiber; 18g protein

SoupTOP
Parmesan Crisps

For the crisps, sprinkle grated Parmesan in a nonstick skillet and toast over medium heat. Use an offset spatula to flip.

Adding ON

Spinach & Salami Salad

Makes 8 cups; Total time: 20 minutes

FOR THE BASIL VINAIGRETTE—
PUREE:

1/2	cup fresh basil leaves
1/4	cup red wine vinegar
1	T. honey
2	t. Dijon mustard
1/4	cup olive oil
	Salt and pepper to taste

FOR THE SALAD—
SAUTE IN 1 T. OLIVE OIL; TOSS WITH:

1/4	lb. salami, julienned
8	cups fresh spinach
1	cup cherry tomatoes, halved
1/2	cup red onion, thinly sliced
1/4	cup Parmesan, shredded
	Basil Vinaigrette

Puree all ingredients for the vinaigrette (except the oil) in a blender. With the blender running, slowly drizzle in the oil until emulsified.

Saute salami for the salad in 1 T. oil over medium heat about 3 minutes, or until crisp; drain on paper towels. Toss the spinach, tomatoes, onion, and Parmesan with the sauteed salami and vinaigrette.

Per cup: 204 calories; 64% calories from fat; 15g total fat; 11g carb.; 510mg sodium; 6g fiber; 11g protein

tortilla SOUP

Wow! This isn't just a bowl of soup—it's a full-blown fiesta in a pot with show-stopping toppings.

Soups like this, with lots of bells and whistles, really excite me. The little extras elevate it to a completely different level.

Take tortilla chips, for example. A lot of times, they're merely a garnish added to justify the soup's name. But here, some are added to the soup to thicken it—they dissolve completely and you don't know they're there, except for the flavor they provide. And naturally, more tortillas are fried to make a garnish!

Tempted to skip the salsa verde on Page 94? Don't do it. It's an easy extra that makes a big difference in flavor.

Tortilla Soup with Chipotle Shrimp

Makes 8 cups

Total time: 1 hour

Char the poblanos (see Tip below), then place them in a plastic bag to steam for easy peeling.

Add the diced tortillas to the soup—they'll dissolve and thicken, adding authentic flavor to the soup.

Rinse the beans before adding them to the soup, then reduce the heat. Simmer to blend flavors.

FOR THE SOUP—

SAUTE IN 2 T. OLIVE OIL; STIR IN:

1½	cups onion, diced
2	T. garlic, minced
1	cup poblano chiles, charred, seeded, and chopped
1	cup frozen corn kernels
1	t. dried oregano
1	t. ground coriander
1	t. ground cumin
¼	t. cayenne

ADD:

4	cups chicken broth
1	can diced tomatoes in juice (15 oz.)
1	can black beans, rinsed and drained (15 oz.)
2	corn tortillas, diced

FOR THE TORTILLA STRIPS—

HEAT:

1	cup vegetable oil
3	corn tortillas, cut into ⅛"-wide strips
	Salt to taste

SERVE SOUP WITH:

Chipotle Citrus Shrimp, *right*
Salsa Verde, *Page 94*

Saute onion and garlic in oil in a large pot over medium-high heat about 5 minutes, or until soft. Stir in chiles, corn, and seasonings.

Add broth, tomatoes, beans, and tortillas. Bring to a boil, reduce heat to low, and simmer 15 minutes. Meanwhile, prepare the tortilla strips and shrimp.

Heat the oil for the tortilla strips to 350° in a saute pan over high. Carefully add tortilla strips in batches and fry about 1 minute, or until crisp and golden. Drain on paper towels and season with salt.

Serve soup with tortilla strips, shrimp, and salsa verde.

Per cup: 217 calories; 49% calories from fat; 12g total fat; 22g carb.; 387mg sodium; 4g fiber; 6g protein

Adding ON

Chipotle Citrus Shrimp

Makes 1 lb. shrimp; Total time: 15 minutes

MELT; ADD AND SAUTE:

2	T. unsalted butter
1	lb. jumbo shrimp, peeled (tails left on) and deveined

STIR IN:

2	T. fresh lime juice
2	T. frozen orange juice concentrate, thawed
1	T. chipotle chile in adobo sauce, minced
	Salt to taste

Melt butter in a saute pan over medium-high heat. Add shrimp and saute 1 minute.

Stir in lime juice, orange juice concentrate, and chipotle. Saute about 3 minutes, or until shrimp is cooked through; season with salt.

Per 2 shrimp: 89 calories; 38% calories from fat; 4g total fat; 1g carb.; 92mg sodium; 0g fiber; 12g protein

SoupTIP

Charring poblanos (or any chile) is a simple task—it's one of the few times you actually want to "char" food! Place them over an open flame or under a broiler until the skin is black and blistered, turning often. Seal in a plastic bag to steam and cool, then peel off the skin.

sausage MINESTRA

If there was ever a "soup for beginners," Sausage Minestra would be it. Simple, fast, and packed with flavor, this soup has only good things going for it.

To put it casually, you get a lot of bang for your buck with this Sausage Minestra. It's embarrassingly easy to make, yet may be one of the best tasting soups to ever cross your lips. This is a terrific blend of hearty flavors and spicy heat, ideal for warming up cool autumn nights.

But here's a word of warning: This soup may be a little on the spicy side for many people. I only use ½ teaspoon of red pepper flakes (that's the stuff you shake on pizza), but they can turn hot on you in a heartbeat. If you're sensitive, cut back on (or omit) the pepper flakes.

Sausage Minestra

Makes 7 cups

Total time: 40 minutes

Saute sausage to brown, then add onion, garlic, and seasonings. Cook until onion turns translucent.

Deglaze with wine, scraping any browned bits from the bottom of the pot. Add broth and tomatoes.

Orzo is a small, rice-shaped pasta. If you can't find it, it's okay to use any small pasta shape.

FOR THE PARMESAN CROUTONS—
TOAST IN 2 T. OLIVE OIL; TOSS WITH:
- 3   cups baguette, cubed
- ½   cup Parmesan, grated

FOR THE SOUP—
SAUTE IN 2 T. OLIVE OIL; ADD:
- 1   lb. link Italian sausage, sliced into 1"-thick pieces
- 2   cups onion, diced
- 1   T. garlic, minced
- 2   t. dried Italian seasoning
- ½   t. kosher salt
- ½   t. red pepper flakes

DEGLAZE WITH; STIR IN:
- ½   cup dry white wine
- 4   cups chicken broth
- 2   cups tomatoes, seeded, diced
- ½   cup dry orzo pasta

STIR IN; SERVE SOUP WITH:
- 3   cups fresh spinach, chopped
  Parmesan Croutons

Toast baguette cubes in oil in a saute pan over medium-high heat until crisp. Off heat, toss with Parmesan; set aside.

Saute sausage in oil in a large pot over medium-high heat until browned. Add the onion, garlic, and seasonings; cook 3–4 minutes, or until the onion is soft.

Deglaze with wine and reduce until almost evaporated. Add broth, tomatoes, and orzo; bring to a boil, reduce heat, and simmer about 10 minutes, or until pasta is cooked.

Stir in spinach until wilted. Serve soup with croutons on top.

Per 1½ cups: 427 calories; 44% calories from fat; 21g total fat; 24g carb.; 186mg sodium; 4g fiber; 34g protein

SoupTIP

Slice sausage into bite-size pieces about 1" thick. Ground sausage may be used but make sure it stays in large chunks.

Adding **ON**

Romaine with Creamy Parmesan

Makes 8 cups; Total time: 10 minutes

WHISK TOGETHER; TOSS WITH:
- 3   T. mayonnaise
- 2   T. Parmesan, grated
- 2   T. fresh lemon juice
- 1   t. Dijon mustard
- 1   t. Worcestershire sauce
    Dash of Tabasco
    Salt and pepper to taste
- 8   cups romaine, torn into bite-sized pieces

GARNISH WITH:
  Parmesan curls

Whisk first 6 ingredients together and season with salt and pepper; toss with romaine.

Garnish with curls of Parmesan.

Per cup: 58 calories; 78% calories from fat; 5g total fat; 2g carb.; 79mg sodium; 1g fiber; 7g protein

chicken
GUMBO

Usually it takes hours to make gumbo, but you can whip this one up in no time. Serve it with French bread for a "Big Easy" dinner—literally and figuratively!

I've made plenty of batches of gumbo in my life, and there are two things that remain constant. First, put your effort into making a good, dark roux [ROO]. Of course, the roux thickens the soup, but it also provides the gumbo's rich color. And more importantly, the dark roux gives the soup a distinctive nutty flavor, a characteristic of all fine gumbos.

The second constant is flexibility. You can put just about anything in gumbo and it will work—crab, shrimp, sausage, oysters, greens...heck, make it vegetarian if you want. Anything goes.

Chicken Gumbo Soup

Makes 12 cups

Brown the chicken and sausage in the soup pot, then remove them. Add the oil and flour for the roux.

Cook the roux carefully, stirring until it has the appearance and aroma of peanut butter.

Simmer the tomatoes, broth, and herbs, then add the okra and reserved meats; simmer gently.

Total time: about 1 hour

BROWN IN 2 T. OLIVE OIL:
- 1 lb. boneless, skinless chicken thighs, cut into 1" pieces
- 8 oz. kielbasa, 1/4"-thick slices

COMBINE; ADD:
- 1/2 cup olive oil
- 1/2 cup all-purpose flour
- 3/4 cup onion, diced
- 3/4 cup green bell pepper, diced
- 3/4 cup celery, diced
- 3 garlic cloves, minced
- 1 t. each cayenne, white pepper, and ground black pepper

STIR IN; SEASON:
- 1 can diced tomatoes in juice (14 1/2 oz.)
- 6 cups chicken broth
- 4 sprigs fresh parsley
- 3 sprigs fresh thyme
- 1 bay leaf
- Salt to taste

ADD:
- 2 cups frozen sliced okra
- Reserved chicken and sausage

Brown chicken and kielbasa in 2 T. oil in a large pot over medium-high heat for 5–8 minutes. Remove meats from the pot and set aside.

Combine oil and flour in the same pot the meat was browned in. Cook, stirring constantly, for about 5 minutes, or until it's the color and consistency of peanut butter. Add the onion, bell pepper, celery, garlic, and seasonings; cook about 5 minutes, or until vegetables are soft.

Stir in tomatoes, broth, and herbs. Simmer 10–15 minutes, then season with salt.

Add okra and reserved meats; simmer 5 minutes. Serve gumbo over steamed white rice if desired.

Per cup: 272 calories; 66% calories from fat; 20g total fat; 11g carb.; 363mg sodium; 1g fiber; 13g protein

Adding **ON**

Mustard Greens & Ham

Makes 3 1/2 cups; Total time: 15 minutes

SAUTE IN 1 T. VEGETABLE OIL; ADD:
- 1/2 cup onion, sliced
- 1/2 cup ham, chopped
- 1 bag frozen chopped mustard greens, thawed (16 oz.)

STIR IN:
- 3 T. white vinegar
- 2 T. sugar
- 1 t. kosher salt
- 1/2 t. red pepper flakes

Saute onion and ham in oil in a saute pan over medium-high heat for 3 minutes. Add greens and cook until heated through, stirring often. **Stir in** remaining ingredients and simmer for 3 minutes.

Per 1/2 cup: 75 calories; 45% calories from fat; 4g total fat; 7g carb.; 412mg sodium; 2g fiber; 4g protein

Soup**TIP**

Roux isn't the only thing that can thicken gumbo: okra and filé are both traditional. Purchase okra fresh or frozen, and don't cook it long or the texture will suffer. Filé (ground dried sassafras leaves) isn't called for here, but should be used sparingly or it will make the gumbo stringy.

vietnamese noodle soup

If Asian food is a foreign affair for you, then this soup is a good starting point.

I'll be willing to bet that after eating it, you'll be ready for more Asian food adventures!

Think of this soup as a *very* loose Asian take on spaghetti and meatballs. Okay, so there's no tomato sauce or cheese, and the pork (not beef) meatballs float in broth with vegetables and noodles. But not all is lost in translation—a bowl of this soup can be just as satisfying as a plate of bolognese!

There are a couple of ingredients in the soup that you may not be familiar with. *Rice noodles* come in several widths, and any size can be used here. But if you'd rather, use cooked vermicelli or ramen. *Fish sauce* is a Vietnamese and Thai staple, but can be substituted with a bit of anchovy paste.

Vietnamese Noodle Soup

Makes 8½ cups   *Total time: 45 minutes*

Brown the meatballs in oil, but don't cook through. They'll finish cooking in the simmering soup.

Add the soy sauce, ginger, sugar, chili garlic sauce, and fish sauce to the simmering broth.

Off heat, stir in the noodles, cabbage, carrot, lemon juice, and sesame oil. Serve soup right away.

FOR THE MEATBALLS—
COMBINE; BROWN IN 1 T. VEGETABLE OIL:

½	lb. ground pork
3	T. scallions, minced
2	T. chopped fresh cilantro
1	T. fresh ginger, minced
1	T. garlic, minced
1	T. soy sauce
1	t. chili garlic sauce
¼	t. each kosher salt and pepper

FOR THE SOUP—
SOFTEN IN BOILING WATER:

¼	lb. rice stick noodles

SIMMER; ADD:

6	cups chicken broth
2	T. soy sauce
1	T. fresh ginger, minced
1	T. sugar
1	t. chili garlic sauce
1	t. fish sauce
	Sauteed meatballs

OFF HEAT, STIR IN:

	Softened rice stick noodles
1	cup napa cabbage, cut into 1" ribbons
½	cup carrot, julienned
1	T. fresh lemon juice
½	t. toasted sesame oil

GARNISH WITH:

¼	cup scallions, sliced on a bias

Combine all meatball ingredients in a bowl; scoop into teaspoon-size balls. Brown in oil in a nonstick skillet over medium-high heat (do not cook through). Transfer meatballs to a plate; chill until ready to use.

Soften noodles in boiling water until pliable, about 15 minutes. Drain, separate clumps with your fingers, and set noodles aside.

Simmer broth, soy sauce, ginger, sugar, chili garlic sauce, and fish sauce in a large pot. Add meatballs and gently simmer just until cooked through.

Off heat, stir in noodles, cabbage, carrot, lemon juice, and sesame oil.

Garnish with scallions and serve.

Per cup: 189 calories; 43% calories from fat; 9g total fat; 17g carb.; 384mg sodium; 1g fiber; 9g protein

SoupTIP

You'll know the meatballs are cooked through when they float in the soup. Don't add the noodles and vegetables to the broth until the meatballs are done. Otherwise, the noodles will soften too much and the vegetables will lose a lot of their texture and bright color.

Adding **ON**

Cucumber Salad

Makes 2 cups; Total time: 20 minutes

TOSS TOGETHER:

2	cups cucumber, seeded, sliced into half-moons
½	cup red onion, slivered
½	cup rice vinegar
1	T. sugar
½	t. red pepper flakes
	Pinch of salt

BEFORE SERVING, GARNISH WITH:

	Chopped dry roasted peanuts

Toss cucumber, onion, vinegar, sugar, pepper flakes, and salt together in a bowl. Marinate for 15 minutes at room temperature.

Before serving, garnish salad with chopped peanuts.

Per ½ cup: 99 calories; 64% calories from fat; 7g total fat; 7g carb.; 116mg sodium; 2g fiber; 4g protein

beef barley soup

Beef barley is one of those soups that can be either really spectacular or really mediocre. This recipe gets top billing due to a few interesting tricks.

Often, a dish can go from okay to outstanding just by applying different techniques to the same ingredients. For example, with this soup, rather than using left-over beef (as is usually the case), short ribs are simmered until tender, then shredded. Yes, this takes longer, but you wind up with succulent beef for the soup *and* a great-tasting soup base. Its

flavor is infinitely better than using canned beef broth, and worth all the time it takes.

Another thing that makes a difference is to cook the barley separately, not in the broth—it'll cloud the soup and absorb too much liquid. Blanch the vegetables separately too. This way, they'll be perfectly cooked in the soup, not over- or underdone.

Beef Barley Soup

Makes 12 cups

Total time: 4 hours

Don't bother trimming the ribs before simmering. Cooked and cooled, the fat is easy to remove.

Blanch the baby vegetables separately until crisp-tender. Then shock in ice water to stop the cooking.

Add the cooked barley to the soup; simmer for a few minutes before serving to heat everything through.

BRING TO A BOIL:
3	lb. beef short ribs
8	cups chicken broth
2	cups water
1/2	t. dried rosemary
2	bay leaves

SIMMER:
4	cups water
3/4	cup barley
	Salt

BLANCH AND SHOCK:
4	oz. baby carrots
1	cup asparagus tips
8	oz. assorted baby summer squash (such as pattypan and zucchini), halved

SAUTE IN 2 T. OLIVE OIL; DEGLAZE WITH AND ADD:
2	cups button mushrooms, quartered
8	oz. shallots, peeled, halved
2	T. garlic, minced
1/2	cup dry sherry
1/2	cup tomatoes, seeded, diced
1	T. minced fresh parsley

Bring ribs, broth, water, and herbs to a boil over high heat in a large pot. Reduce heat to medium-low and simmer 3 hours, or until beef is fork-tender. (Meanwhile, prepare remaining soup ingredients.) Remove ribs and set aside; skim fat from broth, strain, and reserve for the base. When ribs are cool enough to handle, trim fat and gristle, then shred, *see Tip, below.*

Simmer barley in salted water for 40 minutes, or until tender; drain and set aside.

Blanch each type of vegetable separately in boiling water 1–3 minutes (time varies depending on vegetables), or until just tender. Shock in ice water, drain, and set aside.

Saute mushrooms and shallots in oil in a large pot over medium-high heat 3–5 minutes, or until they begin to brown. Stir in the garlic; saute 1 minute. Deglaze with sherry; simmer until nearly evaporated, then add reserved broth (plus enough water, if needed, to yield 6 cups). Add the vegetables, beef, and barley; simmer to heat through. Stir in the tomatoes and parsley, and season with salt and pepper.

Per 1 1/2 cups: 427 calories; 44% calories from fat; 21g total fat; 24g carb.; 186mg sodium; 4g fiber; 34g protein

SoupTIP

Once simmered, the short ribs will be tender enough to "pull" with two forks. Trim off any excess fat or gristle before shredding the beef.

Adding **ON**

Cheddar Biscuits

Makes 10 biscuits; Total time: 40 minutes

MIX TOGETHER; CUT IN:
2 1/2	cups all-purpose flour
1/4	cup sugar
1	T. baking powder
1	t. kosher salt
1/2	t. cream of tartar
6	T. unsalted butter, cold, cubed
1	cup sharp Cheddar, shredded

COMBINE:
1	cup buttermilk
1	egg, beaten

Preheat oven to 450°; line a baking sheet with parchment paper or lightly coat with nonstick spray.

Mix dry ingredients together in a bowl. Cut in butter with a pastry blender or two knives until it's the size of peas; stir in the cheese.

Combine buttermilk and egg in a second bowl, then stir it into the flour mixture just to incorporate. Drop batter onto prepared baking sheet using an ice cream scoop or 1/4-cup measure, spacing 2" apart. Bake biscuits about 15 minutes, or until set and the tops are golden.

Per biscuit: 255 calories; 41% calories from fat; 12g total fat; 30g carb.; 408mg sodium; 1g fiber; 7g protein

beer cheese soup

This soup is another excuse (as if you needed one!) to put beer,

cheese, and brats together. And it doesn't even have to be game day!

The key to great beer cheese soup is balance. The powerful flavors of the beer and cheese have to meet in the middle. Here's what I mean: Dark ales are strong and bitter, and can overwhelm the soup. It's best to use a German lager (such as Heineken), which is more mellow, for the best flavor.

Meanwhile, the cheese has to be robust enough to stand up to the beer. Sharp Cheddar is perfect. It gives this soup its distinctive flavor and color. Be sure to grate the cheese—otherwise it'll take forever to melt. Cream cheese is added to enhance creaminess and smooth out the soup.

Beer Cheese Soup

Makes 6 cups

Sweat vegetables, then add the flour-spice mixture and stir to coat. Cook briefly, stirring often.

Stir in the beer—a light-colored lager is best for this. Darker beers will overpower the soup.

Gradually add cheese, stirring constantly until melted. Do not allow the soup to boil at this stage.

Total time: about 1 hour

SWEAT IN 5 T. UNSALTED BUTTER:
1   cup onion, minced
1/2 cup celery, minced
1/2 cup carrot, minced

COMBINE; STIR IN:
5   T. all-purpose flour
1   t. paprika
1   t. dry mustard

ADD:
1   cup beer (such as lager)
3   cups chicken broth
1   T. Worcestershire sauce
1   t. Tabasco

WHISK IN:
1   cup whole milk
1   lb. sharp Cheddar, grated
4   oz. cream cheese, cubed

STIR IN; SEASON WITH:
2   T. chopped fresh flat-leaf parsley
    Salt to taste

Sweat onion, celery, and carrot in butter in a large pot over medium-low heat for 10 minutes.

Combine flour, paprika, and dry mustard in a bowl, then stir into vegetable mixture. Increase heat to medium and cook 1–2 minutes, stirring often.

Add beer and simmer until thickened. Add broth, Worcestershire, and Tabasco, stirring constantly. Bring to a boil, reduce heat to medium, and simmer 5 minutes.

Whisk in milk and both cheeses, stirring constantly until smooth. Do not boil or the soup may curdle.

Stir in parsley and season with salt.

Per cup: 547 calories; 69% calories from fat; 42g total fat; 17g carb.; 661mg sodium; 1g fiber; 24g protein

Adding **ON**

Sausage-Pumpernickel Skewers

Makes 8 skewers; Total time: 15 minutes

GRILL OR SAUTE; SLICE:
2   bratwurst
SAUTE IN 1/4 CUP OLIVE OIL; THREAD:
16 cubes pumpernickel or marble rye bread (1" squares)
    Cooked bratwurst

Grill or saute bratwurst 8 minutes, or until cooked through, turning often. Slice diagonally into 1"-wide pieces and set aside.

Saute bread in oil in a skillet over medium-high heat for 5 minutes, or until toasted. Alternately thread chunks of bratwurst and bread cubes onto each of 8 skewers.

Per skewer: 203 calories; 59% calories from fat; 13g total fat; 16g carb.; 349mg sodium; 2g fiber; 5g protein

Soup**TIP**

Sometimes boiling is bad. In the case of beer cheese soup, the heat of a rolling boil, around 212°, will cause the cheese to curdle (separate into solids and fats). So to avoid this, it's important to never let the soup come to more than a gentle simmer once the cheese has been added.

oyster chowder

If there's one food that captures the mood of Christmas Eve, it's oyster chowder.

Smooth, rich, warm...this is total splendor without going to a lot of effort.

I used to make oyster chowder with only oysters, cream, and butter. I have to admit, that was simple elegance. But after having it several times at Grand Central Oyster Bar in New York and the Ferry Building in San Francisco, my recipe has changed. While it's still simple, it steps up to a new level.

What makes this chowder special isn't just its flavor, but its great looks too. The simple mirepoix [mihr-PWAH] of carrots, leeks, and celery adds depth to the broth. But since it's simmered for a short period, the vegetables keep their vibrant colors, adding to the soup's visual appeal.

Oyster Chowder

Makes 5½ cups

When sweating the vegetables, it's important to cover the pan to allow steam to soften them.

Simmer the vegetables, uncovered, in the cream and milk until the liquid reduces slightly.

Gently simmer oysters until their edges curl. Take care not to overcook them or they'll turn rubbery.

Total time: 30 minutes

SWEAT IN 4 T. UNSALTED BUTTER; ADD:
2   cups celery, diced
2   cups leeks, sliced, rinsed
ADD:
1½   cups carrot, thinly sliced
1   cup heavy cream
1   cup whole milk
     Salt to taste
STIR IN:
1   pint shucked fresh oysters
     (with liquor)
BRUSH WITH OLIVE OIL; BROIL:
4   baguette slices, ¾" thick
GARNISH WITH:
     Chopped freshly parsley
     Freshly ground black pepper

Preheat broiler to High.
Sweat celery and leeks in butter in a large saute pan over medium-high heat. Cook 3–4 minutes, covered, until the vegetables are translucent and soft.
Add carrots, cream, and milk. Simmer 3–4 minutes, or until slightly thickened; season with salt.
Stir in the oysters and their liquor, reduce heat to medium-low, and simmer 5 minutes.
Brush bread with oil and broil on both sides until golden. Place a slice in the bottom of each serving bowl, then pour the soup over.
Garnish with parsley and pepper. Serve immediately.

Per 1¼ cups: 563 calories; 63% calories from fat; 39g total fat; 37g carb.; 576mg sodium; 3g fiber; 16g protein

Adding ON

Hot Spinach Salad

Makes about 9 cups
Total time: 15 minutes

SAUTE AND REMOVE:
4   strips thick-sliced bacon, diced
COOK IN 1 T. DRIPPINGS; STIR IN:
¾   cup red onion, slivered
¼   cup apple cider vinegar
3   T. honey
1   T. Dijon mustard
     Salt and pepper to taste
OFF HEAT, WHISK IN; TOSS WITH:
⅓   cup olive oil
½   lb. fresh spinach leaves
     Reserved bacon
     Homestyle Croutons, *Page 89*
     Quartered hard cooked eggs,
     optional

Saute bacon in a nonstick skillet over medium-high heat until crisp. Transfer to a paper towel-lined plate; pour off all but 1 T. drippings from the pan and return to burner.
Cook onions in drippings for about 2 minutes—they should remain fairly crisp. Stir in vinegar, honey, mustard, and seasonings. Simmer to reduce slightly, about 1 minute.
Off heat, whisk in oil. Toss dressing with spinach, reserved bacon, croutons, and eggs. Serve immediately.

Per cup: 207 calories; 78% calories from fat; 18g total fat; 9g carb.; 207mg sodium; 1g fiber; 3g protein

SoupTIP

Two things about oysters: First, always pour the liquor (the liquid surrounding oysters) through a mesh strainer to catch stray pieces of shell and sand. Second, don't overcook them! While I said cook for 5 minutes, that's an estimate. They're done when their edges start to curl.

wild rice & chicken soup

There may not be a more welcoming and warming soup than one with chicken and wild rice. Bold, woodsy flavors make it perfect for autumn evenings.

While this wild rice soup is fairly simple, using the right ingredients the right way is important—it's not hard, just critical.

First, use real wild rice (not instant). It has a wonderful nutty flavor, and the texture remains firm and chewy, even when properly cooked, *see Soup Tip, Page 55.*

Second, don't even think about making this soup without good smoky ham and dry sherry ("cream" sherry is too sweet for this dish). And finally, whole milk gives this soup delicate richness without the heaviness of cream. But don't boil the soup once the milk is added, or it could curdle.

Wild Rice & Chicken Soup

Makes about 8 cups

Sweat vegetables with the sauteed ham. This way, the vegetables will soften but won't turn brown.

Add flour and stir to coat vegetables. The flour will lightly thicken the soup and give it some body.

Once the milk is added, don't allow the soup to boil—a gentle simmer is all it needs.

Total time: 45 minutes

SAUTE IN 2 T. UNSALTED BUTTER; ADD:

1	cup ham, diced
1/2	cup onion, diced
1/4	cup carrot, diced
1/4	cup celery, diced

STIR IN; DEGLAZE WITH, THEN ADD:

2	T. all-purpose flour
3	T. dry sherry
4	cups chicken broth
2	cups cooked wild rice
2	cups cooked chicken, chopped
2	t. minced fresh thyme
	Salt and pepper to taste

FINISH WITH; GARNISH SOUP WITH:

1	cup whole milk
1/2	cup scallions, chopped
	Toasted slivered almonds

Saute ham in butter in a large pot over medium heat for 3–4 minutes; add onion, carrot, and celery. Cover, reduce heat to low, and sweat about 5 minutes, or until softened.

Stir in flour to coat vegetables; cook 1 minute, stirring constantly. Deglaze with sherry, scraping up bits from the bottom of the pot. Add broth, cooked rice, chicken, and seasonings. Bring to a boil, reduce heat to medium-low, and simmer 10 minutes.

Finish with milk and scallions. Garnish each serving of soup with toasted almonds.

Per cup: 276 calories; 45% calories from fat; 14g total fat; 18g carb.; 314mg sodium; 2g fiber; 20g protein

Adding **ON**

Fry Bread

Makes 8 rounds; Total time: 45 minutes

BLEND; STIR IN:

1 1/2	cups all-purpose flour
1 1/2	t. baking powder
1/4	t. kosher salt
1	cup warm water

HEAT; FRY DOUGH IN:

1/2	cup vegetable oil, divided

Blend flour, baking powder, and salt in a bowl. Stir in water and knead dough until soft, adjusting flour or water as necessary. Cover and let dough rest 15–20 minutes.

Heat 1/4 cup of the oil in a nonstick skillet over medium-high. Divide dough into 8 pieces and roll on a floured work surface into rounds 4–5" in diameter. Fry in hot oil until puffy and golden on the bottom, then turn and fry on the other side until golden. Drain on a paper towel-lined plate. Fry remaining dough, adding more oil as needed. Serve fry bread warm.

Per fry bread: 203 calories; 61% calories from fat; 14g total fat; 17g carb.; 135mg sodium; 1g fiber; 2g protein

SoupTIP

Wild rice is a long-grain marsh grass that must be rinsed thoroughly before cooking. To cook, bring 2 cups chicken broth, 1 cup water, and 1 1/2 cups wild rice to a boil. Cover and simmer for 50 minutes, or just until tender. Don't overcook—it will continue to cook a bit in the soup.

chicken & crab
CALLALOO

If you haven't had coconut milk in soup before, then definitely give this recipe a try. Loaded with lots of smoky ham, chicken, crab, and chiles, Callaloo is an unusual, hearty Caribbean feast.

Callaloo (or "pepper pot") is one soup that has so much going on, you wonder how it could possibly taste so good. But it does.

The soup's name comes from the leafy greens of the taro plant, which, in the Caribbean, are traditionally added to the pot. Obviously, taro leaves aren't available to most of us, so spinach is used instead. Be sure to add it (and the okra) last so it stays bright green.

Coconut milk is another key ingredient—don't mistake it for the sweeter coconut cream, which is used in mixed drinks.

Chicken & Crab Callaloo

Makes about 9 cups

Cook seasoned chicken and ham in the bacon drippings until the meats begin to brown.

Add onion, garlic, and thyme, and saute until onion is soft. Stir in the broth and simmer.

Don't be alarmed if the coconut milk is solidified when you open the can—just stir the contents to blend.

Total time: 1 hour

SAUTE AND SET ASIDE:

- 4 slices thick-sliced bacon, diced

BROWN; STIR IN:

- 8 oz. boneless skinless chicken breast, cubed, seasoned with salt and pepper
- 1 cup ham, cubed
- 2 cups white onion, diced
- 2 t. garlic, minced
- ½ t. dried thyme leaves
- 6 cups chicken broth

ADD:

- 4 cups fresh spinach, chopped
- 1 cup frozen okra, sliced
- 1 cup coconut milk
  Reserved bacon

STIR IN:

- ½ cup scallions, thinly sliced
- ¼ cup serrano chiles, thinly sliced

DIVIDE AMONG SERVING BOWLS; LADLE SOUP OVER:

- 1 cup pasteurized crabmeat, picked through

Saute bacon in a large pot over medium-high heat until crisp. Drain on a paper towel-lined plate and pour off all but 1 T. of drippings; return pot to the burner.

Brown chicken and ham in the drippings. Stir in onion, garlic, and thyme, and cook, stirring often, about 5 minutes, or until onion is translucent. Add broth, bring to a boil, and reduce heat to low. Cover and simmer 10 minutes.

Add spinach, okra, coconut milk, and reserved bacon; simmer 5 minutes. Season with salt and pepper.

Stir in scallions and serranos.

Divide the crab among serving bowls and ladle soup over.

Per cup: 257 calories; 56% calories from fat; 16g total fat; 12g carb.; 514mg sodium; 4g fiber; 20g protein

SoupTIP

Place crab in the bowls just before serving, then ladle the soup over it. This will keep the crab from breaking down and becoming stringy.

Adding ON

Sticky Rice "Sundaes"
with pineapple salsa

Makes 3 cups rice, 1½ cups salsa
Total time: 25 minutes

FOR THE RICE—

BOIL; STIR IN:

- 2 cups chicken broth
- 1 T. fresh lime juice
- 1 t. brown sugar
  Pinch of ground allspice
  Salt and pepper to taste
- 1 cup medium grain rice

FOR THE SALSA—

STIR TOGETHER:

- 1 cup fresh pineapple, diced
- ¼ cup red onion, diced
- ¼ cup red bell pepper, diced
- 1 T. fresh lime juice
- 1 T. chopped fresh cilantro
- 1 t. brown sugar
  Salt to taste

Boil broth, lime juice, sugar, and seasonings in a saucepan. Stir in rice, cover, reduce heat to low, and cook 15 minutes. Off heat, fluff with a fork, cover, and keep warm.

Stir all salsa ingredients together and serve over scoops of rice.

Per ½ cup rice with ¼ cup salsa: 151 calories; 4% calories from fat; 1g total fat; 33g carb.; 37mg sodium; 1g fiber; 3g protein

POBLANO
corn chowder

The annual appearance of fresh sweet corn is a big deal. But if you want to make it an even bigger deal, whip up this delectable chowder.

Soup in the summertime is a hard thing for people to buy into. But eat this chowder in the middle of August made with ears of fresh sweet corn, and you'll think you've died and gone to heaven. Even with frozen corn, this soup is still worth looking forward to.

Poblano [poh-BLAH-noh] chiles add mild heat that balances the sweetness of the corn. If they aren't available at the grocery store, try a Mexican market. Preparing them is easy—char on all sides over a burner, then steam in a plastic bag until cool and peel off the black skin.

Poblano-Corn Chowder

Makes 8 cups

Saute onion and garlic until onions are translucent. Add broth, corn, and seasonings, then simmer.

Puree half the soup until smooth. Hold the top firmly with a towel and gradually increase speed.

Stir pureed soup back into the pot. Add the chiles and cream; season with salt and cayenne.

Total time: 40 minutes

FOR THE SOUP—
SAUTE IN 2 T. UNSALTED BUTTER:
1   cup white onion, minced
1   T. garlic, minced
ADD; PUREE:
2   lb. fresh or frozen corn
     kernels (6 cups)
4   cups chicken broth
2   t. sugar
FINISH WITH:
2   poblano chiles, roasted,
     peeled, seeded, diced
1/2   cup heavy cream
1 1/2 t. kosher salt
1/2   t. cayenne

FOR THE TOMATO CONCASSÉ—
COMBINE; TOP SOUP WITH:
2   large ripe tomatoes, seeded
     and diced
     Salt and pepper to taste

Saute onion and garlic in butter in a large pot over medium heat. Cook until soft, 3–4 minutes.
Add corn, broth, and sugar. Bring to a boil, reduce heat, and simmer 10 minutes. Carefully puree half the soup (in batches) in a blender, then return the pureed soup to the pot.
Finish with the chiles, cream, and seasonings.
Combine tomatoes and seasonings for the concassé, then dollop some on each serving of soup.

Per cup: 229 calories; 39% calories from fat; 10g total fat; 30g carb.; 504mg sodium; 5g fiber; 7g protein

Adding **ON**

Crab Toasts

Makes 8 toasts; Total time: 25 minutes

MASH TOGETHER; STIR IN:
4   oz. cream cheese, softened
2   T. heavy cream
1/2   cup pasteurized crabmeat
2   T. scallions, minced
2   T. red bell pepper, diced
1/2   t. fresh lemon juice
1   egg yolk
     Salt and cayenne to taste
SPREAD MIXTURE ON AND BROIL;
GARNISH WITH:
4   slices white sandwich bread,
     toasted, halved diagonally
     Chopped fresh chives

Preheat broiler to High.
Mash the cream cheese and cream together until incorporated, then stir in the remaining ingredients (except the bread).
Spread crab mixture on halved slices of bread, being sure to cover the edges (or they'll burn during broiling). Broil on a baking sheet until golden; garnish with chives.

Per toast: 110 calories; 61% calories from fat; 8g total fat; 7g carb.; 146mg sodium; 0g fiber; 4g protein

Soup**TIP**

Fresh corn makes this soup shine, and if you can get some that's chowder-worthy, you'll need about 8 ears to yield the 6 cups needed here. To remove kernels from the cob, stand the ear upright and cut down the cob. Can't get great sweet corn? Don't sweat it—frozen works fine.

baked potato soup

No, your eyes aren't playing tricks on you—that really is steak on top of soup!

Hard to believe? Maybe. But let me tell you, this soup is unforgettable.

While most baked potato soups are pretty good (anything potato is good!), this one goes above and beyond with its garnish—a steak and tomato topping turns soup into dinner! There's no magic here, I just put my favorite foods together. What better pairing than a steak, salad, and baked potato?

It's important to use russet potatoes (a typical baking potato) here. They have a high starch content that thickens the soup, but those starch cells are also able to easily absorb the butter and milk. Of course for an even richer soup, substitute a little cream for some of the milk.

Baked Potato Soup

Makes 7½ cups

Bake the potatoes, then peel. Mash the flesh lightly in a bowl using a potato masher or a fork.

Slowly stir the milk and broth into the flour-coated onion—this way, lumps won't be as likely to form.

Stir in the mashed potatoes, breaking up any big chunks with a spoon. Simmer just to heat through.

Total time: about 1½ hours

FOR THE SOUP—
BAKE:
4   russet potatoes, pierced, rubbed with olive oil, salt, and pepper (about 3 lb.)
SAUTE IN 4 T. UNSALTED BUTTER;
WHISK IN:
½   cup onion, diced
¼   cup all-purpose flour
ADD; STIR IN:
3   cups whole milk
2   cups chicken broth
    Reserved mashed potato flesh (about 4 cups)
    Salt and pepper to taste

FOR THE STEAK—
SEAR AND SLICE:
1   lb. top sirloin steak, 1" thick, seasoned with salt and pepper
SERVE SOUP WITH:
    Sliced steak
    Tomato Relish, *below*

Preheat oven to 450°.
Bake potatoes directly on an oven rack for about 1 hour, or until tender when pierced with a skewer. Cool slightly, then scoop out and lightly mash the flesh; set aside.
Saute onion in butter in a large pot over medium-high heat about 5 minutes, or until soft. Whisk in the flour and cook 2–3 minutes.
Add milk and broth; simmer 4–5 minutes, or until thick. Stir in potatoes and seasonings; simmer 5 minutes. Heat a cast iron skillet over medium-high for 5 minutes.
Sear steak in the hot skillet for 3–4 minutes on one side. Turn and sear the other side 3–4 minutes more (for medium-rare), or until cooked to desired doneness. Remove from the pan, let rest for 5 minutes, then thinly slice against the grain.
Serve soup topped with sliced steak and Tomato Relish.

Per cup: 355 calories; 33% calories from fat; 17g total fat; 28g carb.; 229mg sodium; 3g fiber; 20g protein

SoupTOP
Tomato Relish

COMBINE:
1½   cups tomato, seeded, diced
½   cup blue cheese, crumbled
½   cup chopped fresh chives

Combine all ingredients in a bowl. Chill until ready to serve.

Adding ON

Caesar Salad

Makes 1 cup dressing, 4 cups salad
Total time: 15 minutes

WHISK TOGETHER:
2   T. fresh lemon juice
1   T. mayonnaise
2   t. garlic, minced
½   t. anchovy paste
¼   t. Worcestershire sauce
DRIZZLE IN; ADD:
⅓   cup olive oil
⅓   cup Parmesan, grated
    Salt and pepper to taste
TOSS DRESSING WITH:
4   cups romaine lettuce, chopped
GARNISH WITH:
    Shaved Parmesan curls

Whisk lemon juice, mayonnaise, garlic, anchovy paste, and Worcestershire together.
Drizzle in oil in a steady stream, whisking constantly. Add Parmesan, salt, and pepper.
Toss romaine with enough dressing to coat. (Extra dressing may be chilled for up to 1 week.)
Garnish with Parmesan curls.

Per cup: 144 calories; 86% calories from fat; 14g total fat; 2g carb.; 164mg sodium; 1g fiber; 3g protein

easy, cheesy
BROCCOLI SOUP

I had to do it...an old-school soup made with butter and processed cheese. Yep, it's so good, you can eat the whole batch by yourself.

Try creating a broccoli-cheese soup using "trendy" cheeses—I did, and all I got was a gloppy, grainy mess, nothing like the silky-smooth classic. So why fight it? I know "food snobs" give processed cheese a bad rap, but I'm a food editor who loves the stuff! It's a staple in my fridge at home.

That's not to say that I didn't deviate from the norm a little, though. For one thing, the broccoli florets and stems are blanched separately so they stay crunchy in the soup and aren't cooked to mush. Second, there's no milk added—the cheese gives the soup plenty of body.

Broccoli Cheese Soup

Makes 9 cups

Stir the mirepoix (onion, carrot, and celery) together, then cover the pot and sweat until softened.

Add the cheese, then let it melt into the soup for a minute before stirring—it will incorporate faster.

Add the blanched broccoli a minute or two before serving so it doesn't overcook in the soup.

Total time: 35 minutes

MELT; ADD AND SWEAT:

1   cup onion, minced
1/2   cup carrot, minced
1/2   cup celery, minced

STIR IN; ADD:

2   T. all-purpose flour
4   cups chicken broth

ADD:

1   lb. American cheese, shredded (4 cups)
6   cups broccoli florets and diced stems, blanched
1/4   t. cayenne
     Salt to taste

Melt butter in a large pot over medium heat. Add onion, carrot, and celery; cover and sweat 3 min.
Stir in flour to coat vegetables and cook 1 minute. Slowly add broth, stirring constantly, increase heat to medium-high, then bring to a rolling boil. Cook for 5 minutes, then reduce heat to medium.
Add cheese; let stand 1 minute, then stir until incorporated. Simmer soup for 3 minutes (do not boil, or cheese may curdle), add blanched broccoli, and cook another minute. Season with cayenne and salt.

Per cup: 360 calories; 62% calories from fat; 25g total fat; 18g carb.; 960mg sodium; 5g fiber; 18g protein

Adding ON

Apple & Walnut Salad

Makes 4 cups salad, 1 cup vinaigrette
Total time: 15 minutes

FOR THE VINAIGRETTE—
COMBINE; WHISK IN:

1/4   cup white wine vinegar
1/4   cup olive oil
2   T. chopped fresh chives
1   T. sugar
1   t. kosher salt
1/8   t. cayenne
1/2   cup heavy cream

FOR THE SALAD—
TOAST IN 1 T. UNSALTED BUTTER:

1   cup walnut halves
1   T. sugar
     Pinch of salt

TOSS TOGETHER:

1   Granny Smith apple, cored, thinly sliced
1   cup radicchio leaves, torn
     Sugared Walnuts
     Prepared vinaigrette

Combine vinegar, oil, chives, sugar, and seasonings for the vinaigrette in a bowl; whisk in cream.
Toast walnuts for the salad in butter, sugar, and salt in a small saute pan over medium heat until fragrant, about 3 minutes.
Toss apple, radicchio, walnuts, and about 1/3 cup vinaigrette together. (Remaining vinaigrette may be chilled for up to 1 week.)

Per cup: 376 calories; 84% calories from fat; 35g total fat; 15g carb.; 250mg sodium; 3g fiber; 5g protein

SoupTIP

Don't throw away those broccoli stems! There's plenty of flavor and crunch in the stalks. Peel them with a paring knife, then dice and blanch with the florets.

GINGERED
carrot soup

This has the smoothness and light body you expect in a meatless soup,

but its intense flavor may take you by surprise—pleasantly.

I'll admit, I'm usually the first to turn my nose up at anything tagged as "vegetarian." I just like the satisfying flavor of meat. But this pureed carrot soup is no lightweight. The fresh ginger really brings out the sweetness of the carrots, and pureeing brings them together beautifully.

To get as rich and smooth a texture as possible, it's important that the carrots are sliced thin and are about the same size so they cook evenly. Also, be sure they're completely tender before pureeing—after simmering, fish out four or five carrots and taste them. If all are soft, you're set.

Gingered Carrot Soup

Makes 4 cups soup, 1½ cups tangy cream   Total time: 35 minutes

Add the carrots to the sauteed leeks—be sure they're sliced thin and an equal size for even cooking.

The acidity of the wine adds depth to the sweet carrots. You may use unsweetened apple juice if desired.

A hand blender works great for pureeing, but you can also use a regular stand blender.

FOR THE SOUP—

SAUTE IN 2 T. UNSALTED BUTTER; ADD:

1	cup leeks, sliced and rinsed
1	T. fresh ginger, minced
1	t. garlic, minced

STIR IN AND SAUTE:

1	lb. carrots, peeled, thinly sliced
1	t. sugar
½	t. kosher salt
¼	t. cayenne

DEGLAZE WITH; STIR IN, THEN PUREE:

½	cup dry white wine
3	cups chicken broth

FINISH WITH:

1	T. fresh lemon juice

FOR THE TANGY CREAM—

WHIP; FOLD IN:

½	cup heavy cream
½	cup sour cream
	Salt to taste

Saute leeks in butter in a large pot over medium-high heat about 3 minutes, or until soft. Add ginger and garlic, and cook 1 minute.

Stir in carrots, sugar, salt, and cayenne; saute 1 minute.

Deglaze with wine and reduce until nearly evaporated, then stir in the broth and bring soup to a boil. Reduce heat and simmer 5 minutes, or until carrots are soft. Puree with a hand blender.

Finish soup with lemon juice.

Whip cream to soft peaks in a bowl, then fold in the sour cream and salt. Dollop onto servings of soup.

Per cup with 2 T. cream: 242 calories; 56% calories from fat; 15g total fat; 18g carb.; 418mg sodium; 4g fiber; 5g protein

Adding **ON**

Carrot Raisin Salad

Makes 2 cups; Total time: 20 minutes

STIR TOGETHER:

¼	cup fresh lemon juice
3	T. chopped fresh parsley
2	T. olive oil
2	t. honey
¼	t. ground cinnamon
	Minced zest of 1 lemon
	Salt to taste

ADD:

2	cups carrots, shredded
½	cup raisins
¼	cup scallions, sliced
¼	cup pistachios, chopped

Stir the lemon juice, parsley, oil, honey, cinnamon, zest, and salt together in a bowl.

Add the remaining ingredients (except pistachios) and toss to coat. Sprinkle with nuts before serving.

Per ½ cup: 212 calories; 46% calories from fat; 11g total fat; 28g carb.; 76mg sodium; 4g fiber; 3g protein

SoupTIP

Carrots are so ubiquitous to cooking that we hardly give them much thought. But for this soup, use firm, bright orange carrots that are as fresh as you can find. Avoid using baby carrots here—they're not as sweet, nor do they have the nutritional properties of larger carrots.

clam chowder

New England tradition and modern convenience come together here, making this chowder rich, thick, and undeniably delicious.

The cast of characters in this clam chowder recipe is straight-forward: salt pork, clams, potatoes, and half and half. But "conveniences" (canned clams and bottled clam juice) make this soup a viable, yet flavorful option for busy cooks.

It's worth seeking out the salt pork for this. Salt pork, a fatty piece of salted, unsmoked pork, is traditional in chowder, but if you can't find it, saute a few bacon strips instead (two or three strips is all—you don't want to mask the sweetness of the clams). Before cooking, score the salt pork so fat renders out.

Fresh in-the-shell clams are a gorgeous addition to the soup. But you'll still get plenty of "clammy" flavor from just two cans of prepared clams.

Clam Chowder

Makes 8½ cups

Score the salt pork to resemble a porcupine, then saute it until ¼ cup of fat is rendered.

This chowder is full of clams—both minced and chopped. Don't over-cook, or they'll turn rubbery.

If using fresh clams, be sure they're well scrubbed, then add them at the same time as the canned.

Total time: about 1 hour

SIMMER:

4	cups Yukon gold potatoes, peeled and cubed
3	cups chicken broth
	Pinch of salt

RENDER AND REMOVE; ADD:

8	oz. salt pork, scored
1½	cups onion, diced
½	cup celery, sliced

SPRINKLE IN; STIR IN AND SIMMER:

¼	cup all purpose flour
1	cup chicken broth
1	bottle clam juice (8 oz.)
2	bay leaves
2	fresh thyme sprigs
¼	t. ground white pepper

FINISH WITH; GARNISH SOUP WITH:

1	can minced clams drained and rinsed (6½ oz.)
1	can chopped clams, drained and rinsed (6½ oz.)
5	lb. fresh small clams, such as littlenecks or cherrystones, scrubbed, *optional*
1	cup half and half, warmed
	Tabasco to taste
	Bacon Bread Crumbs, *left*

Simmer potatoes, 3 cups broth, and salt in a large saucepan about 10 minutes, or until potatoes are tender. Drain in a colander over a bowl, reserving cooking liquid and potatoes.

Render salt pork in a large pot over medium-high heat until about ¼ cup of fat is in the pot; remove pork and discard. Add onion and celery, and sweat about 5 minutes, or until soft.

Sprinkle in flour, stir to coat vegetables, and cook 1 minute. Stir in 1 cup broth, clam juice, seasonings, and reserved potato cooking liquid. Simmer 5 minutes, or until thick.

Finish with reserved potatoes, clams, half and half, and Tabasco; adjust salt and pepper as needed. Return soup to a simmer and cook for 3 minutes (if using fresh clams, cook until they open; discard any unopened clams). Garnish with crumb topping.

Per cup: 307 calories; 39% calories from fat; 13g total fat; 34g carb.; 516mg sodium; 2g fiber; 12g protein

SoupTOP
Bacon Bread Crumbs

SAUTE; ADD:

4	strips thick-sliced bacon, minced
1	cup coarse bread crumbs

OFF HEAT, TOSS WITH:

1	T. minced fresh parsley
1	t. minced lemon zest
	Salt and pepper to taste

Saute bacon until crisp, remove, and drain. Add crumbs to drippings; saute about 5 minutes, or until toasted, stirring often.

Off heat, toss crumbs and reserved bacon with remaining ingredients.

Adding **ON**

Vinegar Slaw

Makes 3 cups
Total time: 15 minutes + chilling

BRING TO A BOIL:

¼	cup white wine vinegar
¼	cup sugar

WHISK TOGETHER; TOSS WITH:

	Vinegar mixture
3	T. mayonnaise
2	T. heavy cream
½	t. dry mustard
	Salt to taste
1	pkg. prepared coleslaw mix (12 oz.)
¼	cup chopped fresh parsley

Bring vinegar and sugar to a boil in a small saucepan over medium-high heat, stirring to dissolve. Boil 3 minutes; cool for 5 minutes.

Whisk vinegar mixture, mayonnaise, cream, mustard, and salt in a large bowl. Toss dressing with coleslaw mix and parsley; cover and chill 1 hour before serving.

Per ½ cup: 296 calories; 23% calories from fat; 8g total fat; 47g carb.; 466mg sodium; 0g fiber; 0g protein

cheeseburger SOUP

Cheeseburger Soup started out as a playful idea, but ended up a staff hit. It's got everything a good burger should—a little fun and a whole lot of flavor!

Who'd have imagined that a classic diner blue plate special could morph so successfully into a bowl of soup? Of all the recipes in this book, this one might be the king of comfort—with fries "on the side," even!

This basic cheese soup is built on vegetables and browned hamburger. Ground sirloin's lower fat content helps keep the soup from getting greasy. As for cheese, I use sharp Cheddar because of its flavor, but mild Cheddar or American works too.

Don't skip over the Shoestring Fries and pickle garnishes! Besides adding flair to the recipe, they pump up the soup's flavor.

Cheeseburger Soup

Makes 8½ cups

Total time: 35 minutes

Brown beef in butter, breaking it up with a spoon. Add vegetables, saute, then add broth and potatoes.

Make the flour-milk mixture, then stir it in to the soup and bring to a simmer. Cook until thickened.

The ketchup and mustard add to the fun and flavor of this soup. Stir them in at the end.

Soup**TOP**
Shoestring Fries

Cut peeled russets into thin strips; heat ½" vegetable oil to 350°. Fry potatoes until golden, drain, and sprinkle with salt.

BROWN IN 1 T. UNSALTED BUTTER; ADD:

1	lb. ground sirloin
1	cup onion, diced
¾	cup celery, diced
½	cup carrot, diced
1	t. garlic, minced

STIR IN:

3	cups chicken broth
2	cups russet potatoes, peeled, diced
1	t. dried basil

MELT; WHISK IN:

3	T. unsalted butter
¼	cup all-purpose flour
1½	cups whole milk

ADD; SERVE WITH:

2	cups Cheddar cheese, grated
¼	cup ketchup
2	T. prepared yellow mustard Salt and pepper to taste Shoestring Fries and chopped dill pickles

Brown beef in 1 T. butter in a large pot over medium heat. Cook until the meat begins to brown, then add the onion, celery, carrot, and garlic. Saute about 10 minutes.

Stir in the broth, potatoes, and basil; bring to a boil, reduce heat, and simmer 10–12 minutes, or until potatoes are cooked through.

Melt 3 T. butter in a saucepan over medium heat. Whisk in flour and cook 1–2 minutes, then add the milk, whisking until smooth, scraping the bottom of the pan. Add the milk mixture to the soup and bring to a boil. Reduce heat to a simmer.

Add cheese, ketchup, mustard, salt, and pepper, stirring until the cheese is melted. Serve with fries and chopped pickles.

Per cup: 305 calories; 53% calories from fat; 18g total fat; 17g carb.; 379mg sodium; 1g fiber; 21g protein

Adding **ON**

Chopped Salad

Makes 6 cups salad, 1 cup dressing
Total time: 10 minutes

FOR THE "SPECIAL SAUCE" DRESSING—
WHISK TOGETHER:

¼	cup white wine vinegar
¼	cup olive oil
¼	cup mayonnaise
2	T. ketchup
1	T. sweet pickle relish
1	t. prepared horseradish Salt to taste

FOR THE SALAD—
TOSS TOGETHER; DRIZZLE WITH:

4	cups romaine or iceberg lettuce, chopped
1½	cups tomatoes, chopped
½	cup onion, sliced Prepared dressing

Whisk all ingredients for the dressing together and set aside.

Toss lettuce, tomatoes, and onion together, then drizzle with dressing. (Leftover dressing may be refrigerated for up to 1 week.)

Per cup: 106 calories; 75% calories from fat; 9g total fat; 7g carb.; 82mg sodium; 2g fiber; 1g protein

bay CIOPPINO

Seafood soups don't have to be labor intensive and difficult to prepare.

The secret is to use fresh seafood and make a quick, flavorful base.

Cioppino [chuh-PEE-noh] is a San Francisco icon. This is a special soup, packed with seafood in a spicy tomato broth, and is similar to France's bouillabaisse. Cioppino is easier to make than the long-cooking French version, yet just as impressive when ladled into big, shallow bowls.

And substitutions are allowed, so don't get hung up if you can't find the fish listed in the recipe. It's fine to use any similar seafood your fishmonger has to offer, as long as it's super-fresh. Any good white fish works, and you can substitute crab for shrimp or clams for mussels.

Bay Cioppino

Makes about 10 cups

To build layers of flavor, sweat vegetables until soft, then add tomato paste, seasonings, and wine.

Add chunks of fish and mussels to the simmering soup. Partially cover and cook just until mussels open.

Add shrimp and cook just until firm. Don't overcook or the fish will dry out and the shrimp will be tough.

Total time: 1 hour

SWEAT IN 2 T. OLIVE OIL:
- 1   cup onion, sliced
- 1/2   cup carrot, sliced
- 1/2   cup celery, sliced
- 1/2   cup yellow bell pepper, sliced
- 1/2   cup fresh fennel bulb, cored, sliced
- 1   T. garlic, minced

STIR IN; DEGLAZE WITH:
- 2   T. tomato paste
- 1   T. chopped fresh thyme
- 2   t. chopped fresh oregano
- 1   t. red pepper flakes
- 1   t. kosher salt
- 1   bay leaf
- 1 1/2   cups dry white wine

ADD:
- 1   can whole tomatoes with juice, chopped (28 oz.)
- 2   cups chicken or clam broth
- 2   T. fresh lemon juice
- 1   t. sugar

STIR IN; ADD:
- 1   lb. mussels, cleaned and debearded
- 3/4   lb. cod or other firm white fish, cut into 1 1/2" cubes
- 1/2   lb. medium shrimp, peeled, tails left on, deveined, seasoned with salt and pepper

GARNISH WITH:
- 3   T. chopped fresh parsley

Sweat onion, carrot, celery, bell pepper, fennel, and garlic in oil in a large pot over medium heat. Cook for 5 minutes, stirring often.

Stir in tomato paste, herbs, and seasonings, and saute 2 minutes. Deglaze with wine; simmer about 5 minutes, or until reduced by half.

Add tomatoes, broth, lemon juice, and sugar. Bring to a simmer and cook 10 minutes.

Stir in mussels and cod; simmer 5 minutes, discarding mussels that do not open. Add shrimp and simmer 3–4 minutes, or until cooked through and firm.

Garnish soup with parsley.

Per 1 1/4 cups: 230 calories; 23% calories from fat; 6g total fat; 13g carb.; 695mg sodium; 2g fiber; 23g protein

SoupTIP

Store mussels in a bowl in the refrigerator covered with a damp towel. To use, pull off the scraggly "beard" with your fingers or pliers, then scrub with a nylon brush and wash in several changes of cold water. Discard mussels with broken shells or any that don't open after cooking.

Adding **ON**

Sourdough Panzanella

Makes 8 cups; Total time: 20 minutes

TOAST IN 2 T. OLIVE OIL:
- 4   cups sourdough bread cubes (1" cubes)

WHISK TOGETHER; ADD:
- 1/3   cup white wine vinegar
- 1/4   cup olive oil
- 1   T. shallot, minced
- 1/2   t. Dijon mustard
- 1/2   t. sugar
- 2   cups tomatoes, chopped
- 1   cup cucumber, seeded and chopped
- 1/2   cup yellow bell pepper, diced
- 1/2   cup kalamata olives, pitted, sliced
- 1/4   cup red onion, slivered
- 1/4   cup torn fresh basil leaves
- 1/4   cup whole fresh flat-leaf parsley leaves
- 2   T. capers, drained
  Salt and pepper to taste

Toast bread cubes in 2 T. oil in a skillet over medium-high heat.

Whisk vinegar, 1/4 cup oil, shallot, Dijon, and sugar together in a large bowl. Add bread and remaining ingredients; toss to coat. Season with salt and pepper.

Per cup: 194 calories; 65% calories from fat; 14g total fat; 15g carb.; 353mg sodium; 2g fiber; 3g protein

chicken pot pie soup

Who doesn't like pot pie? It's a throwback to simpler times when food cured all kinds of ailments. Here's a fast version for a quick pick-me-up to heal any wounds.

While it's reminiscent of the pot pies of old, this recipe bucks tradition, turning all those flavors you remember into a soup. It's still thick and rich with the same vegetables as the original. But there's one thing this soup *is* missing—time invested in the kitchen. And who's got a problem with that?

There are a couple of things that will slash your kitchen time. First, forget making a pie crust. I know, it's one of the best parts, but puff pastry croutons are just as good, and quick too. Second, use rotisserie chicken. Once it's in the soup, no one will know the grocery store cooked it for you!

Chicken Pot Pie Soup

Makes about 8½ cups

Total time: 45 minutes

Sprinkle flour over sweated vegetables; stir constantly to coat and to prevent the flour from scorching.

Add the chicken and seasonings to the soup—leftover or rotisserie chicken works great here.

Stir in the peas and parsley just before serving. Otherwise, their color will fade.

SWEAT IN 4 T. UNSALTED BUTTER; STIR IN:

1	cup onion, diced
1	cup celery, diced
1	cup button mushrooms, quartered
½	cup carrot, diced
2	t. garlic, minced
1½	cups red potatoes, diced
¼	cup all-purpose flour

DEGLAZE WITH; STIR IN:

2	T. dry sherry
5	cups chicken broth
2	cups cooked chicken, shredded
2	T. chopped fresh thyme
1	bay leaf
½	t. kosher salt
¼	t. black pepper
	Pinch of ground nutmeg

ADD:

½	cup frozen corn kernels
½	cup frozen green peas
2	T. chopped fresh parsley
2	t. fresh lemon juice
	Salt and pepper to taste

Sweat onion, celery, mushrooms, carrot, and garlic in butter in a large pot over medium-high heat. Cook 3–4 minutes, then stir in potatoes and cook 3 more minutes. Whisk in flour; cook 1–2 minutes.

Deglaze with sherry, then stir in the broth, chicken, and seasonings. Bring to a boil, reduce heat to medium, and simmer 10–15 minutes, or until thickened.

Add corn, peas, parsley, and lemon juice. Season with salt and pepper.

Per cup: 212 calories; 40% calories from fat; 9g total fat; 17g carb.; 252mg sodium; 2g fiber; 15g protein

Adding **ON**

Puff Pastry Croutons

Makes 2 cups; Total time: 25 minutes

ROLL OUT; BEAT TOGETHER AND BRUSH OVER:

1	sheet purchased puff pastry, thawed
1	egg
1	T. water

SPRINKLE WITH:

Kosher salt, paprika, and grated Parmesan

Preheat oven to 450°; line a baking sheet with parchment paper.

Roll pastry out on a lightly floured work surface to ¼" thick. Beat egg with water, then brush over dough.

Sprinkle dough lightly with salt, paprika, and Parmesan, and cut into 1½" squares. Transfer to the prepared baking sheet and bake 15–20 minutes, or until golden.

Per ¼ cup: 42 calories; 55% calories from fat; 3g total fat; 3g carb.; 177mg sodium; 0g fiber; 2g protein

SoupTIP

Puff pastry is a French delicacy made by rolling cold butter into multiple layers of dough. When baked, the butter melts and creates steam, causing the dough to puff into hundreds of thin, flaky layers. Use a pizza wheel to cut the unbaked puff pastry sheet into squares.

BRUNSWICK STEW

A southern favorite, Brunswick Stew takes common ingredients and puts them together to create a spicy, sweet, barbecue-flavored stew. It's perfect anytime.

Maybe you've heard of Brunswick Stew, a tomato-based, slowly simmered stew that was originally made with...squirrel! Well, don't worry, this recipe doesn't have anything wild in it, just chicken and plenty of colorful vegetables. It's so good that I make a double batch and freeze some for later.

This stew nearly cooks itself—prepackaged ingredients make it a quick deal. I use rotisserie chicken, but you could also cook pieces. I recommend thighs since they're juicier and more flavorful than breast meat. Don't like lima beans? Leave them out. The stew is perfectly fine without them.

Brunswick Stew

Makes 12 cups

Saute bacon, then cook the onion and garlic in the drippings. Deglaze with the broth, then add tomatoes.

After simmering the broth base, stir in the chicken and seasonings, then simmer another 20 minutes.

Finish the stew with the beans and corn. You may use canned white beans instead of the limas.

Total time: about 1 hour

SAUTE:
- 3   strips thick-sliced bacon, diced
- 2   cups onion, diced
- 1   T. garlic, minced

DEGLAZE WITH; ADD:
- 3   cups chicken broth
- 1   can diced tomatoes with juice (28 oz.)

STIR IN; SIMMER:
- 2   lb. cooked chicken, chopped
- 1   cup ketchup
- 1/2   cup brown sugar
- 1/4   cup prepared yellow mustard
- 1/4   cup Worcestershire sauce
- 1/4   cup apple cider vinegar
- 1   T. Tabasco
-     Juice of 1 lemon

ADD:
- 2   cups frozen lima beans
- 2   cups frozen corn kernels

Saute bacon over medium-high heat in a large pot until bacon begins to turn crisp. Add onion and garlic, and saute about 4 minutes, or until onion begins to soften.

Deglaze with broth, scraping up any brown bits from the bottom of the pot. Add the tomatoes and simmer 25 minutes.

Stir in the chicken, ketchup, brown sugar, mustard, Worcestershire, vinegar, Tabasco, and lemon juice. Bring to a simmer and cook an additional 20 minutes.

Add the lima beans and corn, simmer 5 more minutes, then serve.

Per cup: 200 calories; 16% calories from fat; 4g total fat; 31g carb.; 638mg sodium; 3g fiber; 12g protein

SoupTIP

Since rotisserie chicken is a quick alternative to roasting your own bird (and fairly inexpensive), it's used in a lot of these soup recipes. Don't pitch the drippings in the tray—add them to the stew for flavor.

Adding ON

Mini Corn Muffins

Makes 12–14 muffins; Total time: 35 minutes

WHISK TOGETHER:
- 1/2   cup all-purpose flour
- 1/2   cup yellow cornmeal
- 1/2   t. baking powder
- 1/2   t. kosher salt
- 1/4   t. baking soda

COMBINE; ADD TO DRY INGREDIENTS:
- 1/2   cup buttermilk
- 1/2   cup canned cream-style corn
- 1/2   cup sharp Cheddar, shredded
- 1   egg, lightly beaten
- 2   t. vegetable oil
- 1   T. jalapeño, seeded, minced

Preheat oven to 425°; coat a mini-muffin pan with nonstick spray.

Whisk first 5 ingredients together in a large bowl.

Combine remaining ingredients in another bowl, then add to dry ingredients, stirring just to incorporate. Spoon batter into prepared muffin pan, filling cups 3/4 full. Bake 18–20 minutes, or until golden brown and a toothpick inserted in the center comes out clean. Cool muffins in the pan for 1 minute, then remove and cool on a rack.

Per muffin: 82 calories; 34% calories from fat; 3g total fat; 11g carb.; 273mg sodium; 1g fiber; 3g protein

lasagna SOUP

This lasagna soup is made for a weeknight warm-up. It tastes like its seven-layered cousin, but takes half the time and a fraction of the work.

During last year's holiday feeding frenzy, I pulled out all the stops. I smoked turkeys, made stuffings, roasted prime rib, and baked pies until I could cook no more. Afterwards, I was inundated with recipe requests—but not for the fancy food. People wanted *this* recipe that I served the night *before* the festivities!

Not that I'm disappointed anytime anyone asks for a recipe, but after using every culinary trick I knew, I thought they'd be more interested in the elaborate dishes. So to me, that tells the whole story. This lasagna soup is quick, simple, satisfying, and packed with flavor—just ask anyone in my family.

Lasagna Soup

Makes 8 cups

Saute the sausage, onion, and carrot, then stir in the mushrooms and garlic.

Add the broth and tomatoes, then bring soup to a boil before stirring in the uncooked pasta.

Ladle soup over cheese to melt. For best results, wait briefly to serve so the cheese has a chance to soften.

Total time: 45 minutes

BROWN; STIR IN:

1	lb. ground Italian sausage
2	cups onion, chopped
1	cup carrot, diced
2	cups button mushrooms, sliced
2	T. garlic, minced

ADD; STIR IN:

4	cups chicken broth
1	can chopped Italian-style stewed tomatoes (14 1/2 oz.)
1	cup mafalda pasta, *see below*
2	cups fresh spinach, chopped

SERVE SOUP OVER; GARNISH WITH:

1	cup provolone or fresh mozzarella, diced
1/4	cup Parmesan, shredded
4	t. thinly sliced fresh basil

Brown sausage in a large saucepan over medium-high heat. Add onion and carrot; saute 3 minutes. Stir in mushrooms and garlic, and saute another 3 minutes.

Add broth and tomatoes; bring to a boil. Stir in the pasta and simmer until cooked, about 10 minutes (or according to package directions). Add the spinach and cook about 1 minute, or until wilted.

To serve, place cubes of cheese in each serving bowl, then ladle soup over to melt. Garnish with Parmesan and basil.

Per cup: 309 calories; 53% calories from fat; 18g total fat; 20g carb.; 943mg sodium; 3g fiber; 11g protein

SoupTIP

If you can't find mafalda (mini lasagna noodles), substitute campenelle pasta. Cooking the pasta in this soup will thicken and enrich the broth.

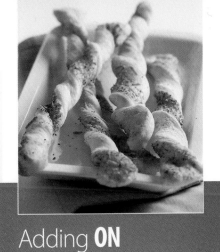

Adding **ON**

Spiced Parmesan Twists

Makes 12 twists; Total time: 25 minutes

COMBINE:

2	T. Parmesan, shredded
1	t. kosher salt
1	t. ground black pepper
1/2	t. garlic powder
1/4	t. paprika

UNROLL; BRUSH AND SPRINKLE WITH:

1	tube refrigerated breadstick dough (11 oz.)
1	T. olive oil
	Parmesan spice mixture

Preheat oven to 375°; line a baking sheet with parchment paper.

Combine Parmesan and seasonings in a small bowl.

Unroll dough onto a lightly floured surface (do not separate into breadsticks yet). Brush with oil and sprinkle cheese mixture evenly over the top.

Separate dough at perforations, then grasp both ends of each piece and gently stretch to 10–12" long. Twist into a spiral and arrange on the prepared baking sheet 1/2" apart. Bake 15 minutes, or until golden; cool breadsticks on a rack for 3 minutes before serving.

Per twist: 90 calories; 29% calories from fat; 3g total fat; 13g carb.; 374mg sodium; 0g fiber; 3g protein

peanut
sweet potato

The first time I heard of this soup, I had a hard time believing I'd like it. But after

one bite, it became one of my new favorites—it may become one of yours too.

Sweet and salty are two flavor facets that pair better than any out there, and this soup proves it. Don't let its unique ingredient list fool you—this really is one of the best soups you'll ever eat.

Like most soups, this one starts out by sauteing the "aromatics" (onion and garlic). What makes it different at this stage is the addition of chili powder and cayenne. Sauteing the spices a bit helps tame their "raw" flavors. But take care not to burn them, or they'll impart a harsh, bitter taste to the soup.

Stirring peanut butter into soup isn't something you'll do everyday, but the richness and flavor it provides is really remarkable. If you don't have creamy peanut butter on hand (my pantry is always stocked with super-chunky), don't panic. Chunky varieties work fine and add a little bonus texture!

Peanut Sweet Potato Soup

Makes 8 cups

Saute the spices with the onion and garlic. Stir frequently to prevent the spices and garlic from scorching.

Dice the sweet potato fairly small so it cooks quickly, but be careful that it doesn't cook to mush.

Stir the peanut butter into the soup—the heat will melt it so it disperses through the broth.

Total time: 45 minutes

SAUTE IN 2 T. VEGETABLE OIL:
1	cup onion, diced
1	T. garlic, minced
1	T. chili powder
1	t. kosher salt
$^1/_2$	t. cayenne

ADD:
$^1/_2$	cup carrot, diced
$^1/_2$	cup celery, diced
$^1/_4$	cup red bell pepper, diced
2	cups sweet potatoes, peeled, diced

STIR IN:
4	cups chicken broth
2	cups cooked chicken, shredded
1	can diced tomatoes in juice (14$^1/_2$ oz.)
$^1/_2$	cup creamy peanut butter

GARNISH WITH:
Chopped dry roasted peanuts
Minced fresh cilantro

Saute onion, garlic, and seasonings in oil in a large pot over medium heat. Cook until onion is slightly softened, about 5 minutes.
Add carrot, celery, bell pepper, and sweet potato; saute 2–3 minutes.
Stir in broth, chicken, tomatoes, and peanut butter. Bring to a boil, reduce heat, and simmer 10 minutes, or until potatoes are tender.
Garnish soup with chopped peanuts and cilantro.

Per cup: 260 calories; 52% calories from fat; 15g total fat; 16g carb.; 571mg sodium; 3g fiber; 17g protein

Adding **ON**

Jicama Slaw

Makes 2½ cups; Total time: 15 minutes

PREPARE:
2	cups jicama, peeled, shredded
$^1/_2$	cup carrot, shredded

TOSS WITH:
$^1/_4$	cup rice vinegar
2	scallions, sliced on a bias
2	T. fresh lime juice
1	t. sugar
1	t. chili garlic sauce
	Salt to taste

Prepare jicama and carrot, shredding each in a food processor or on a box grater; transfer to a bowl.
Toss with remaining ingredients; serve at room temperature or chilled.

Per ½ cup: 32 calories; 3% calories from fat; 0g total fat; 8g carb.; 26mg sodium; 3g fiber; 1g protein

SoupTIP

Jicama [HEE-kah-mah] isn't in the soup, it's in the salad side dish which is a lovely textural contrast to the soup. Jicama looks like a flattened softball covered with a thick, tan skin. Once peeled, the flesh looks similar to a potato but tastes like a cross between celery and apple.

caldo verde

Portuguese cuisine isn't well known over here, but this soup is just one of many great dishes from the country. Try it—you'll understand why it's so popular.

It's hard to believe, but this soup has just three primary players—pepperoni, potatoes, and kale. Which just goes to show that it doesn't take a laundry list of ingredients (or a lot of time) to make a terrific soup.

Traditional caldo verde is made with linguiça [lihng-GWEE-suh], a Portuguese sausage. It's hard to find so I use pepperoni for its similar texture and flavor (thin slices of kielbasa work too). To render out some of the fat, saute it before adding to the soup.

Kale is a rugged winter green that holds up well in the hot broth. Collard or mustard greens make good substitutes, though.

Caldo Verde Soup

Makes 11 cups

Saute the potatoes in the oil to coat. Stir often to keep them from scorching on the bottom.

Once the potatoes are cooked through, coarsely mash them a bit to give the broth a little more body.

To prevent the soup from turning greasy, saute the pepperoni and drain it before adding to the broth.

Total time: 45 minutes

SAUTE IN ¼ CUP OLIVE OIL; STIR IN:

2½ lb. russet potatoes, peeled, sliced ⅛" thick

2 cups onion, diced

½ t. red pepper flakes

ADD; DEGLAZE WITH AND STIR IN:

1 T. garlic, minced

¼ cup Madeira or dry sherry

6 cups chicken broth

SAUTE AND ADD; STIR IN:

½ lb. pepperoni, sliced into half-moons

4 cups kale, stemmed and chopped

Salt to taste

SERVE WITH:

Lemon wedges

Saute potatoes in oil in a large pot over medium heat. Cook 3–5 minutes, or until potatoes begin to brown. Stir in onion and pepper flakes; cook 5 minutes, or until onion softens.

Add garlic and saute 1 minute, then deglaze with Madeira, scraping the bottom of the pot. Simmer until liquid is nearly evaporated. Stir in broth, bring to a boil, reduce heat, and simmer 10–15 minutes, or until potatoes are cooked through. When the potatoes are soft, use a potato masher to crush the slices and thicken the soup. Don't overcrush—the potatoes should retain some texture.

Saute pepperoni in a nonstick skillet over medium-low heat in 2 batches to render some of the fat. Drain pepperoni on paper towels, then add to soup. Stir kale and simmer 2–3 minutes; season with salt.

Serve soup with lemon wedges.

Per cup: 276 calories; 51% calories from fat; 16g total fat; 25g carb.; 437mg sodium; 2g fiber; 9g protein

Adding ON

Shrimp Toasts

Makes 4 toasts; Total time: 20 minutes

COMBINE:

10 medium shrimp, cooked, deveined, chopped (4 oz.)

4 oz. goat cheese, crumbled

¼ cup scallions, sliced

Salt and cayenne to taste

TOAST; TOP WITH AND BROIL:

4 slices ciabatta, ½" thick

Shrimp mixture

Preheat broiler to High.

Combine shrimp, cheese, scallions, salt, and cayenne in a bowl.

Toast ciabatta slices on a baking sheet under the broiler. Divide mixture among bread, then broil 1–2 minutes, or until cheese browns.

Per toast: 126 calories; 48% calories from fat; 7g total fat; 7g carb.; 127mg sodium; 0g fiber; 9g protein

SoupTIP

Strip the kale leaves off the stems by running your hand down the length of the stem. Chop the leaves; discard the stems.

RED CHILI

I know, everyone has a favorite chili and theirs is "the best." So is mine. But after tasting this one, I bet you'll add it to your recipe box like I have.

For this special soup book, I figured there was no way I could leave out chili. But could I make a remarkable bowl of red when *everyone* has a recipe? Yes! What I did was borrow good ideas from a bunch of great-tasting chili recipes and blended them together. The result was outstanding!

The base for this chili is roughly similar to how some big-time chili cookoff winners do things—they often use cubed beef, lots of chili powder, and beef broth. But then it takes a different turn: masa harina (corn flour used for making tortillas) is added for thickening and flavor.

Red Chili

Makes 8 cups

Saute the cubed beef to sear, then add the sausage, crumbling it into the pot with your fingers.

Cooking the seasonings in the broth mixture allows them to "bloom" in the chili.

Masa harina, a main ingredient in corn tortillas, is a great thickener and flavor enhancer for the chili.

Total time: 1 hour

SAUTE IN 3 T. OLIVE OIL; ADD:

1	lb. chuck roast, diced
1/2	lb. ground Italian sausage
2	cups onion, diced
1	cup green bell pepper, diced
2	T. garlic, minced

STIR IN AND SIMMER; ADD:

3	cups beef broth
1	can diced tomatoes with juice (14½ oz.)
3	T. chili powder
1	T. dried oregano
2	t. ground cumin
1/4	t. cayenne

ADD:

1	can kidney beans, drained and rinsed (15 oz.)
1/4	cup masa harina
	Salt and pepper to taste

GARNISH WITH:

Shredded Cheddar
Sour cream
Chopped scallions

Saute beef in oil in a large pot over high heat about 3 minutes, or until seared. Reduce heat to medium-high and add the sausage; saute about 3 more minutes, or until browned. Add onion, bell pepper, and garlic; saute 5 minutes.

Stir in broth, bring to a boil, and simmer 15 minutes. Add tomatoes and seasonings, then simmer an additional 20 minutes.

Add beans and masa, and cook about 10 minutes, or until beef is tender and chili is thickened. Season with salt and pepper.

Garnish servings of chili with cheese, sour cream, and scallions.

Per cup: 404 calories; 51% calories from fat; 23g total fat; 22g carb.; 506mg sodium; 5g fiber; 27g protein

Adding **ON**

Spicy Corn Cakes

Makes 10 cakes
Total time: about 20 minutes

STIR TOGETHER; FRY:

1	cup yellow cornmeal
1	T. jalapeño, seeded and minced
1	t. kosher salt
1¼	cups boiling water
4	T. vegetable oil, divided

Stir cornmeal, jalapeño, salt, and water together in a bowl. Heat 2 T. oil in a nonstick skillet over medium-high, then drop 2 T. batter for each cake into the pan. Flatten slightly and fry on both sides 2–3 minutes, or until golden; remove and drain on a paper towel-lined plate. Continue frying, adding 1 T. oil as needed.

Per cake: 92 calories; 54% calories from fat; 6g total fat; 10g carb.; 363mg sodium; 1g fiber; 1g protein

Soup**TIP**

Two things: First, I'm pretty loose with my chili criteria, so of course you can use ground beef rather than diced chuck. And second, you don't have to use masa harina. A couple of small corn tortillas will do the trick, too, but add them at the same time as the tomatoes.

chili verde

A bowl of chili doesn't have to be red. This pork-based version of a south-of-the-border classic is a great reason to "go green."

Most people define chili as a tomato-based, bean-and-meat concoction. Chili verde, on the other hand, is another deal altogether. Half of its color and flavor comes from tomatillos [tohm-ah-TEE-ohs], the tart, husk-covered, pale green tomato-like fruit.

Its other color and flavor partner is Anaheim chiles. For this they're oven-roasted, not charred, which concentrates their sugars. The chiles, as well as the tomatillos, can easily be picked up at Mexican markets, but many grocery stores have begun to stock them too.

Chili Verde

Makes 7 cups

Roast chiles on a parchment-lined baking sheet. Flip them halfway through the roasting time.

The tequila adds flavor and helps loosen the bits on the bottom of the pot; much of the alcohol burns off.

This chili gets much of its green color from tomatillos ("verde" means "green" in Spanish).

Total time: 1½ hours

ROAST:
6   Anaheim chiles

SEAR IN 2 T. VEGETABLE OIL:
1½   lb. pork steak, trimmed and cut into 1" pieces

DEGLAZE WITH; ADD AND SWEAT:
2   T. tequila
3   cups white onion, diced
2   cups tomatillo, diced
3   T. garlic, minced
1   T. ground cumin
2   t. dried oregano
1   t. ground coriander
1   t. kosher salt

STIR IN:
3   cups chicken broth
     Roasted chiles

FINISH WITH:
1   T. fresh lime juice
     Pico de Gallo, *Page 95*

Preheat oven to 400°.

Roast chiles in the oven for 20 minutes, flipping halfway through. Transfer to a bag to steam for 10 minutes, then peel, remove the stems and seeds, and chop.

Sear pork in oil in a large pot over high heat until browned.

Deglaze with tequila, scraping up bits from the bottom of the pot. Add onion, tomatillo, garlic, and seasonings. Sweat over medium heat, stirring often, for about 10 minutes, or until onion softens.

Stir in broth and chiles. Bring to a boil, reduce heat to low, and simmer 30 minutes.

Finish with lime juice. Top servings of chili with Pico de Gallo.

Per cup: 280 calories; 42% calories from fat; 13g total fat; 15g carb.; 402mg sodium; 2g fiber; 22g protein

SoupTIP

Pork steaks are cut from the shoulder blade roast (also called Boston roast). It's a less tender cut, which makes it perfect for long-simmering soups. These steaks are loaded with fat—remove as much as you can before searing.

Adding ON

Gouda Nachos
with Avocado Crema

Makes 6 oz. nachos, 1 cup crema
Total time: 15 minutes

FOR THE NACHOS—
ARRANGE ON BAKING SHEET AND SPRINKLE WITH; BROIL:
6   oz. corn tortilla chips
2   cups Gouda cheese, grated

FOR THE CREMA—
PUREE:
1   ripe avocado, halved, pitted, and peeled
½   cup sour cream
1   T. fresh lime juice
     Salt to taste

Preheat broiler to High; coat a baking sheet with nonstick spray.

Arrange chips for the nachos in a single layer on the prepared baking sheet; sprinkle with cheese. Broil about 1 minute, or until cheese melts.

Puree all ingredients for the crema in a blender or food processor until smooth. Serve on the side with the nachos.

Per oz. chips with 2½ T. crema: 280 calories; 67% calories from fat; 21g total fat; 13g carb.; 247mg sodium; 4g fiber; 10g protein

PAN-TOASTED Ciabatta
rubbed with garlic & tomato

Forget squishy garlic bread made with margarine and garlic powder. This stuff is the real deal, perfect for dunking into a bowl of hot soup.

Once you've had this crispy, pungent garlic toast, you'll have a tough time with what's usually billed as "garlic bread." The rubbed-on garlic really permeates—a few strokes on each slice is plenty. The optional tomato rub-down is a Spanish thing (called *pan con tomate*) and a very good idea indeed. With a super-ripe red tomato it's astoundingly delicious.

Pan-toasted Ciabatta
Makes 8 slices; Total time: 20 minutes

TOAST IN 2 T. OLIVE OIL:
8   slices ciabatta, 1/2" thick
RUB WITH; SPRINKLE WITH:
2   garlic cloves, halved
1   Roma tomato, halved, *optional*
    Kosher salt

Toast half the bread in 1 T. oil in a large saute pan over medium-high heat. Cook about 5 minutes, or until golden on both sides. Remove and toast the remaining bread in the additional tablespoon of oil.
Rub one side of the warm bread with the cut sides of the garlic cloves. If desired, rub the same side with the cut portion of the tomato; sprinkle with salt.

Per slice: 59 calories; 59% calories from fat; 4g total fat; 5g carb.; 118mg sodium; 0g fiber; 1g protein

BREAD on the side

With or without the tomato, this pan-toasted bread is great with nearly every soup in the book! But it's a natural with the Tuscan Minestrone (Page 16) or the Turkey Tortellini (Page 38). And there's no reason why it wouldn't taste terrific with a big bowl of spaghetti!

PARMESAN **Baguette**
baked with garlic butter

Who doesn't like cheesy garlic bread? This version with herb-heavy garlic butter is so good, you'll be dreaming up excuses to make it!

Garlic cheese bread isn't new, but I've had enough below-average renditions to know that *this* is how it should be! Starting with a good baguette is imperative—the crust should be sturdy but not rock-hard. And really *toast* the bread, or you'll miss the flavor that browning imparts.

Parmesan Baguette
Makes 1 baguette; Total time: 20 minutes

COMBINE; SPREAD OVER:

1	stick unsalted butter, softened
2	garlic cloves, minced
2	t. minced fresh parsley
1	t. kosher salt
1/4	t. dried oregano
1/4	t. paprika
1/4	t. red pepper flakes
1	baguette, halved lengthwise
1/2	cup Parmesan, shredded

Preheat oven to 425°.

Combine butter, garlic, parsley, and seasonings in a bowl. Spread cut sides of baguette with butter mixture and sprinkle with Parmesan. Place bread, buttered side up, on a baking sheet lined with a cooling rack. Bake for 10 minutes, or until cheese and bread are toasted.

Per 1/12: 115 calories; 70% calories from fat; 9 total fat; 5g carb.; 302mg sodium; 0g fiber; 3g protein

BREAD on the side

Once again, this is a recipe that's inherently universal—it works with most of the soups here. Of course, anything tomato-based is great with it, but the Cioppino (Page 70) and Caldo Verde (Page 80) are especially good pairings, as is linguine with marinara or clam sauce.

PESTO Cheese Bread
with fresh mozzarella

Melt cheese on bread and you've got a winner, no matter what. But this pesto-laced loaf is one for the record books!

Easy to execute and delicious in its simplicity, you'll find yourself making this soup side over and over.

Decent bread is of utmost importance—ciabatta [chyah-BAH-tah] is perfect because of its chewy interior and crisp crust. The pesto on Page 97 is great, but if you're strapped for time, don't feel guilty if you opt to use a purchased variety.

BREAD on the side

Because of the rich mozzarella, serve this substantial bread alongside brothy soups. Try it with the Red Bean and Chard Soup (Page 22) or the Italian Wedding Soup (Page 32). The loaf is also great as an accompaniment to a green salad dressed with a tangy vinaigrette.

Pesto Cheese Bread
Makes 1 loaf; Total time: about 20 minutes

HALVE LENGTHWISE; SPREAD WITH:

1   ciabatta loaf
      Basil Parsley Pesto, *Page 97*

TOP WITH:

8   oz. fresh mozzarella, cut into
      1/2"-thick slices

Preheat oven to 450°.

Halve ciabatta lengthwise. Spread pesto over cut sides of both halves.

Top each half with 4 slices of mozzarella and arrange the halves on a baking sheet lined with a cooling rack. Bake bread for 15 minutes, or until cheese begins to brown.

Per 1/12: 161 calories; 68% calories from fat; 12g total fat; 6g carb.; 248mg sodium; 1g fiber; 6g protein

BREAD on the side

*In the case of these croutons, the question might be, "What **don't** they taste good in?" Float them in a bowl of Roasted Tomato Soup (Page 18) or the Split Pea with Ham (Page 34). Or toss them with any number of the salad sides in this book. You just can't go wrong!*

HOMESTYLE Croutons
with herbs and spices

Got bread? Got 10 minutes? Then you can make croutons! And really, you should—these beat any store-bought version, hands down. You'll never go back to the box.

I'm all about using convenience products from time to time, but I draw the line at croutons. Homemade ones taste so much better, and there's always a loaf of bread around to use. Inexpensive French bread works well—its soft crust makes for croutons that are easy on the dental work!

Homestyle Croutons
Makes 4 cups; Total time: 10 minutes

COMBINE:
1	t. kosher salt
1	t. garlic powder
1/2	t. dried basil
1/4	t. paprika

HEAT; ADD AND TOAST:
1/3	cup olive oil
4	cups bread cubes (cut into 1" squares)

Combine seasonings in a bowl. **Heat** oil in a large nonstick skillet over medium-high. Add bread cubes and saute until toasted, about 5 minutes, stirring often. Toss croutons with seasonings while they are still warm.

Per 1/4 cup: 63 calories; 70% calories from fat; 5g total fat; 4g carb.; 164mg sodium; 0g fiber; 1g protein

beef
KEBABS

Beef Rumaki
Makes 8 kebabs; Total time: 25 minutes

ASSEMBLE KEBABS WITH:

½ lb. sirloin steak, trimmed, cut into eight 1–2" pieces, seasoned with salt and pepper

8 slices canned water chestnuts

4 scallions, halved

4 strips thick-sliced bacon, halved crosswise

BASTE WITH:

¼ cup purchased teriyaki sauce

Preheat the grill (or a stovetop grill pan) to medium.

Assemble kebabs by placing one slice of water chestnut and one scallion half on a piece of seasoned beef. Wrap a strip of bacon around the vegetables and beef, then thread with a bamboo skewer to secure. Grill kebabs 4–5 minute per side, or until bacon is crisp.

Baste both sides of each kebab generously with teriyaki sauce and cook another minute longer.

Per kebab: 82 calories; 41% calories from fat; 4g total fat; 4g carb.; 289mg sodium; 0g fiber; 7g protein

Skewers **ON THE SIDE**

It might seem like an odd pairing, but these Japanese-inspired kebabs work surprisingly well with the French Onion Soup (Page 20). Try it!

chicken
SKEWERS

Skewers ON THE SIDE

The tropical flavors of these kebabs are delightful with the Black Bean Soup (Page 10) or the Gingered Carrot Soup (Page 64).

Jerk Chicken Kebabs
Makes 8 kebabs; Total time: 30 minutes

MARINATE; ASSEMBLE KEBABS WITH:
- 1/2   lb. boneless, skinless chicken breast, cut into eight 1–2" pieces
- 1/4   cup Pickapeppa-brand hot sauce
        Salt and pepper
- 1   orange, cut into 8 wedges

MELT; BRUSH KEBABS WITH:
- 1/4   cup sweet orange marmalade

Preheat the grill (or a stovetop grill pan) to medium.

Marinate chicken in Pickapeppa sauce for about 10 minutes; season with salt and pepper. Assemble kebabs, threading each with a piece of chicken and an orange wedge. Grill about 4 minutes per side, or until chicken is cooked through.

Melt the marmalade in a saucepan over low heat. Remove kebabs from the grill and brush with melted marmalade before serving.

Per kebab: 91 calories; 34% calories from fat; 3g total fat; 10g carb.; 67mg sodium; 0g fiber; 5g protein

fruit
SKEWERS

Pineapple-banana Bowties
Makes 8 kebabs; Total time: 20 minutes

ASSEMBLE KEBABS WITH:

1   fresh pineapple, peeled, cored, quartered lengthwise, and cut into 16 wedges, about 1" thick

1   slightly underripe banana, sliced into 1" chunks

WHISK TOGETHER; BASTE WITH:

1/4   cup honey

1   T. Sriracha hot sauce

2   t. minced fresh mint

Preheat the grill (or a stovetop grill pan) to medium.

Assemble each of 4 kebabs with 2 wedges of pineapple and a chunk of banana, starting and ending with a pineapple wedge (arrange them so the pineapple wedges "hug" the banana).

Whisk the honey, Sriracha, and mint together in a bowl. Coat grill with nonstick spray, then grill kebabs 5–7 minutes, turning once. Off heat, baste with honey sauce.

Per kebab: 75 calories; 1% calories from fat; 0g total fat; 20g carb.; 24mg sodium; 1g fiber; 1g protein

Skewers **ON THE SIDE**

This "fire and ice" fruit skewer gets finished with a sweet, spicy sauce that has just a hint of fresh mint. Serve it alongside the Chicken Pho Ga (Page 36) or the Peanut Sweet Potato Soup (Page 78). Or, skip the spicy sauce altogether and serve the warm grilled skewers with vanilla ice cream!

shrimp
KEBABS

Herb Grilled Shrimp
Makes 4 kebabs; Total time: 25 minutes

MINCE TOGETHER; STIR IN:

1/4	cup onion, diced
3	T. chopped fresh parsley
1	T. chopped fresh basil
1	garlic clove
1/4	cup olive oil
2	T. white wine vinegar
1/2	t. kosher salt
1/4	t. ground black pepper
1/4	t. red pepper flakes

ASSEMBLE KEBABS WITH:

8	jumbo shrimp, peeled, tails left on, deveined

Preheat the grill (or a stovetop grill pan) to medium.

Mince the onion, parsley, basil, and garlic together either by hand or in a food processor. Stir in the oil, vinegar, and seasonings; set aside.

Assemble kebabs by threading 2 shrimp on each of 4 skewers. Grill 3–5 minutes per side, or until shrimp are cooked through. Off heat, baste with the herb mixture.

Per kebab: 87 calories; 76% calories from fat; 7g total fat; 2g carb.; 263mg sodium; 0g fiber; 3g protein

Skewers ON THE SIDE

These simple skewers are great with so many of the soups, but they go particularly well with the Spanish Gazpacho (Page 26) and the Poblano Corn Chowder (Page 58). Or serve on their own with Salsa Verde (Page 94).

salsa VERDE

In my book, you never can have too many condiments in your arsenal. This herby sauce is just the ticket for jazzing up all kinds of foods.

"Salsa verde" is Spanish for green sauce, and there are countless recipes for this bright green condiment—but the only common thread among them is their color. This one is heavy on cilantro, which is kept in check with some parsley. The sauce keeps for several days in the fridge, but expect its color to fade a bit due to the acid in the lime juice.

Salsa Verde

Makes ¾ cup; Total time: 10 minutes

PUREE:

2	cups fresh cilantro leaves
1	cup fresh flat-leaf parsley leaves
¼	cup scallions, chopped
¼	cup fresh lime juice
¼	cup olive oil
	Salt and red pepper flakes to taste

Puree all ingredients in a blender or food processor until smooth. (Keeps for up to 1 week chilled.)

Per tablespoon: 49 calories; 88% calories from fat; 5g total fat; 2g carb.; 9mg sodium; 1g fiber; 1g protein

SAUCES on the side

This sauce livens up almost anything with ties to Mexican or Latin American cooking, as well as some Asian dishes. It's stirred into the Tortilla Soup (Page 40), but try it with the Black Bean Soup too (Page 10). Or spoon it over thinly sliced grilled flank steak—muy delicioso!

pico de GALLO

Fresh pico de gallo is more than just a partner for tortilla chips.
It's an unusual, flavorful topping for soups too!

Pico de gallo ("rooster's beak" in Spanish) is so common nowadays it seems silly to make it. But homemade pico is tons better than store-bought options and super-easy to make. Use the freshest ingredients you can get.

Pico de Gallo

Makes about 1 cup
Total time: 15 minutes

TOSS *TOGETHER:*

1	cup tomatoes, seeded, diced
1/4	cup white onion, minced
2	T. minced fresh cilantro
1	T. fresh lime juice
1	jalapeño, seeded, diced
	Salt to taste

Toss all ingredients together in a bowl; chill until ready to serve. (Keeps 1–2 days chilled.)

Per 1/4 cup: 13 calories; 15% calories from fat; 0g total fat; 3g carb.; 5mg sodium; 0g fiber; 1g protein

SAUCES on the side

A spoonful of cool pico de gallo on a bowl of warm soup, like the Black Bean (Page 10), is an interesting contrast between hot and cold, smooth and crunchy. The pico is great on quesadillas, of course, but it's also excellent served over a piece of grilled halibut.

romesco SAUCE

When it comes to using this sauce, there's no end to the possibilities. Subtly sweet and slightly spicy, this may become your new "ketchup."

If you haven't tried romesco sauce, put it on your to-do list, soon! This Spanish sauce is a cinch to make, and so flavorful that you'll be tempted to dab it on almost anything.

If you're short on time, it's fine to use canned roasted peppers. And if you happen to have sherry vinegar, by all means use it here—it's traditional, as are the almonds.

Romesco Sauce
Makes ¾ cup; Total time: 10 minutes

PULSE:

1	red bell pepper, roasted, peeled, seeded, diced
¼	cup olive oil
¼	cup slivered almonds, toasted
¼	cup Parmesan, shredded
2	T. white wine vinegar
	Salt and red pepper flakes

Pulse all ingredients in a food processor until sauce-like. (Keeps for up to 1 week chilled.)

Per tablespoon: 73 calories; 85% calories from fat; 7g total fat; 1g carb.; 82mg sodium; 0g fiber; 2g protein

SAUCES on the side

This is one of my favorite sauces—it's hard to imagine anything that it won't improve! Drizzle this romesco over the Butternut Squash Soup (Page 12) or use as a spread on a roasted chicken sandwich or grilled hamburger. Cold poached shrimp are great dipped in it as well.

basil parsley
PESTO

Sure, it's easy to find tubs of basil pesto at the grocery store. But it doesn't hold a candle to straight-from-your-kitchen pesto!

This pesto recipe is a little different than most. Yes, it has basil, but its flavor is toned down a bit with parsley. And the pine nuts are toasted first to eliminate their "raw" flavor. Toast the nuts in a skillet over medium heat, stirring frequently, until golden. But be careful—they burn in a heartbeat.

Basil Parsley Pesto
Makes ⅔ cup; Total time: 5 minutes

PUREE:

1	cup packed fresh basil leaves
½	cup fresh flat-leaf parsley leaves
¼	cup olive oil
3	T. Parmesan, grated
2	T. pine nuts, toasted
2	garlic cloves
¼	t. red pepper flakes
	Minced zest and juice of 1 small lemon
	Salt to taste

Puree all ingredients in a food processor until smooth. (Keeps for up to 1 week chilled; may also be frozen for up to 1 month.)

Per tablespoon: 41 calories; 88% calories from fat; 4g total fat; 1g carb.; 2mg sodium; 0g fiber; 0g protein

SAUCES on the side

Stir a little of this pesto into the Tomato and Turkey Tortellini Soup (Page 38) or use on the Garlic Pesto Bread (Page 88). It's also great to have on hand to spread over a pizza crust or toss with pasta—try it with penne, cooked green beans, and boiled new potatoes!

splendid SOUPS recipe index